THIS SIDE OF *Glory*

This Side of Glory: Celebrating 25 Years of Higher Things

Published by:
1517 Publishing
PO Box 54032
Irvine, CA 92619-4032

Publisher's Cataloging-in-Publication
(Provided by Cassidy Cataloguing Services, Inc.)

Names: Higher Things (Organization), author.
Title: This side of glory : celebrating 25 years of Higher Things / Higher Things.
Description: Irvine, CA : 1517 Publishing, [2026]
Identifiers: ISBN: 9781967920174 (paperback) | 9781967920181 (ebook)
Subjects: LCSH: Higher Things (Organization)—History. | Religious institutions—United States—History. | Christian education—United States—History. | Congresses and conventions—United States—History. | Lutheran Church. | LCGFT: Essays. | BISAC: RELIGION / Christianity / Lutheran. | RELIGION / Christian Church / General. | RELIGION / Christian Theology / General.
Classification: LCC: BV1463 .H54 2026 | DDC: 268.0973—dc23

Printed in the United States of America.

Cover art by Julie Meyer.

THIS SIDE OF *Glory*

CELEBRATING 25 YEARS OF HIGHER THINGS

A CURATED COLLECTION OF ESSAYS FROM HIGHER THINGS

Table of Contents

Foreword

Rev. Marcus Zill

"If then you were raised with Christ, seek those things which are above, where Christ is, sitting at the right hand of God. Set your mind on things above, not on things on the earth."
~ Colossians 3:1-2

What's in a Name?

People have always taken the task of naming someone, or something, new rather seriously ever since God gave Adam the authority and high privilege to "name" that which He had created (Genesis 2:19-20). Names are important. They speak to identity. They get to the core of who someone is or what something is to be about. In many ways, you are who you are named. God's name is so important that the Second Commandment makes it clear that we are not to misuse it.

The biblical record is filled with the accounts of how seriously the naming of people is taken, including times God would change someone's name in order to establish, or highlight, their new identity.

God changed Abram's name, "exalted father," to "Abraham," meaning "father of many nations" (Genesis 17:5), and Sarai from "princess" to Sarah, the "mother of nations" (Genesis 17:15-16). That promise was fulfilled through Isaac, whose son, Jacob, was given the name Israel, meaning "one who struggles with God" (Genesis 32:28).

In the New Testament, Jesus changed Simon's name to Peter, meaning "rock," to emphasize that the foundation of Christ's church would be built on Peter's confession that Jesus was the "Christ, the Son of the Living God" (Matthew 16:17-18).

The angel Gabriel, which fittingly means "God is my strength", gave the Virgin Mary the exact name at the Annunciation for her to call her son: *"And behold, you will conceive in your womb and bring forth a Son, and shall call His* name JESUS" (Luke 1:29).

The name JESUS is the transliteration of the Hebrew "Yeshua," which means "Yahweh saves" or "Yahweh is salvation." The very name, Jesus, was rooted in Christ's divine purpose as the Son of God and Son of Man.

Of course, even beyond the biblical examples, which are too numerous to mention here, every married couple that is expecting their first child will undoubtedly be given a baby name book. They will spend countless hours pondering what name to give each of their children. They will look at it from every angle, ponder what the name means, listen to how it sounds, and perhaps reflect on who it might honor. And, of course, it is with the very name given to you that you are baptized into Christ.

Yes, there is a lot in a name. A name helps create one's identity and serves as a reinforcement of that identity. The same is also true for an organization like Higher Things because, once again, to name something is ultimately to speak to its purpose, or in the case of an organization, its identity.

The funny thing is that the name Higher Things was at first a simple play on words by a young campus pastor in Laramie, Wyoming, in the spring of 1999. It turns out that when you live at 7,220 feet, you quickly learn that everyone must have a little bit of fun developing phrases and naming things relative to living at such a high elevation. For instance, in Wyoming, it was common to joke about looking down at Nebraska, being at a much lower elevation, and all over campus at the University of Wyoming that year were signs and bumper stickers that said things like, "Cowgirl volleyball. Volleyball with an altitude!"

I pondered some rather silly things, like having a campus ministry tagline like "St. Andrew's Lutheran Church & Campus Center: The Divine Service with an Altitude!" Yeah, that one seemed like a winner when it first rolled off my tongue, but it didn't land well in real life. Not to be deterred, I began searching the Scriptures for references to things like height and altitude for inspiration. I wanted to capture what I thought our campus ministry should all be about going forward, and of course, if possible, still have something to do with elevation.

I eventually came across the Colossians passage (3:1-2) in which Paul reminded us to focus on things above, and not on things below, and thought, "Aha. Higher Things." That's what we should be about—Higher Things!

That became the new name of our campus ministry newsletter (yes, people still created things like that on paper back then in the late 90s!). Following the Dying to Live National Lutheran Youth Conference in 2000, when Higher Things itself was eventually founded and, yes, named, let's just say, I ended up having to find a new name for my campus ministry newsletter.

So yes, one could say, Higher Things got its beginning at 7,220 feet, that is, high elevation. But that wouldn't be the whole story. After all, people didn't gather in Laramie, Wyoming, that summer just to be at a high elevation, but they clearly did come together to focus on, and receive, things from above.

But what is Higher Things? Is it an organization? Is it a series of conferences? Is it a ton of biblical and catechetical content, or is it a philosophy of all those things? Simply put, yes. Ultimately, it's about being properly vertically aligned and having your priorities ordered accordingly. The name Higher Things reminds you that you are not citizens of this world and that your identity is found in Christ.

Colossians 3:1-2 has certainly served as a wonderful theme verse ever since. However, when you ponder it more closely, since the Bible is a book of salvation, all of God's revealed Word, from beginning to end, is ultimately about "higher things." For example:

While the priest and the Levite passed by on the other side of the man bleeding and left for dead in the ditch, the Good Samaritan alone focused on things from above and had compassion (Luke 10:25-37).

When Mary anointed the Lord's feet with oil and Judas grumbled (John 12:1-8), she was focused on higher things, just as when she chose to sit at Jesus' feet and learn (Luke 10:38-42) rather than helping her sister Martha, who grumbled that she wasn't helping her serve.

After the ten lepers were healed, the one returned and fell on his face at the feet of Jesus, knowing that Jesus was the source of higher things (Luke 17:15-16).

Certainly, the devil and the world and our sinful flesh tempt us continually to focus on lower things:

The devil's temptation in the Garden of Eden was to get Adam and Eve to focus on lower things and believe that God was only keeping the higher things for Himself (Genesis 3).

Jesus Himself was tempted unsuccessfully by the devil for forty days to focus on lower things until Jesus eventually said, *"Be gone Satan! For it is written, 'You shall worship the Lord your God and Him only shall you serve'"* (Matthew 4:1-11).

Our Lord was always focused on higher things for the sake of the world. On the night when He was betrayed, Jesus prayed in another garden, the Garden of Gethsemane, *"Father, if you are willing, remove this cup from me. Nevertheless, not my will, but yours be done"* (Luke 22:42). Jesus as the Son of God and Son of Man was truly the very embodiment of higher things who for the joy that was set before Him endured the cross, despised its shame, and is seated at the right hand of the throne of God (Hebrews 12:2).

And certainly, when Jesus ascended above, the two angels told the disciples not to stand and gaze looking into heaven and reminded them that Christ would return (Acts 1:11), but that Christ would soon send the Holy Spirit as promised at Pentecost and *"clothe them with power from on high"*(Luke 24:49).

The point? In a way, your whole life will be a variation on this theme of focusing on higher things. This shouldn't surprise us. Jesus Himself reminded us to have this proper vertical discipline in our lives when He told us the following:

> *"Seek first the kingdom of God and His righteousness, and all these things will be added unto you."*
> ~ Matthew 6:33

Look, you will have a lot of "things" to do in this life, including your various God-given vocations. But the challenge will be to keep them in the proper alignment, not to be anxious, not to serve mammon instead of God, and to trust that He will provide for you. It's only when the things of this life are ordered rightly toward God that they, in fact, can benefit us and our neighbor, too. No wonder we are reminded in the explanation to the First Commandment that "We are to fear, love, and trust in God above all things." Go figure.

Jesus Himself tells us to seek not the things that are below, but the things that are above. The point is that your life is not to be consumed by such things below but to be seeking after things above. The direction of your life is to first be toward Him and His righteousness. This doesn't mean that you don't do what each day gives you to do, but don't let it consume you. Invest in the things above that will never perish, and not in the things below that will.

So, in the early days of Higher Things, we sought to invest in helping young people do just that. And we took the following phrase by Gordon Dahl in his book, *Work, Play, and Worship in a Leisure-oriented Society* (1972) to heart, namely that in our culture everything is wrongly aligned:

"We worship our work, work at our play, and play at our worship."

We accepted the challenge to help others reverse that so that they can remain focused on what matters most, on higher things. Since the organization's inception, we have focused on making worship, real worship; making study, real study; and making fun, real fun. Higher Things has always strived to be the level best at all three, while keeping them in the right order and not confusing them as if they are all one and the same. Priorities.

We have always strived to keep Higher Things about just that—higher things. We have unashamedly always focused on doctrine. Why? Because doctrine is about the very words of Christ. And we have focused intently as well on our liturgical practices, that is, how you receive that Holy Word. We have always followed what was embodied in the fifth-century Latin expression, *lex orandi, lex credendi*. What does this mean? It means that "the rule of prayer or of worship is the rule of faith." Simply put, our life of worship shapes what we believe, and vice versa. The way we worship affects the way we believe. Or, to put it another way, practice teaches doctrine.

The Holy Scriptures that God caused prophets, apostles, and evangelists to write are about focusing our attention on higher things from beginning to end. They also serve as a reminder that when the Lord ascended on high, he did not leave us on earth alone with "no" things. No, He gave us higher things. We have His spoken Word and Absolution, the Gift of Holy Baptism, and even the edible forgiveness that we receive in His Body and Blood in the Sacrament.

Those higher things have served His church well and sustained it while we await His return from above:

When the disciples left what they were doing to follow Christ (Matthew 16:24), and they and the early church martyrs refused to denounce Christ or die, they chose higher things.

The Lutheran Reformation itself was about retaining these higher things in the church where "the Gospel is rightly taught, and the Sacraments are rightly administered" (AC IV. The Church).

When the Saxon immigrants and other confessional Lutherans came to the United States in the nineteenth century, they were seeking refuge in a place where they would still have the freedom to keep their focus on higher things.

And when you confirmed your faith and made a vow to suffer all, even die, rather than fall away from the faith (LSB, p.272ff), you committed yourself to these things above, too.

In line with those who have come before us, it is our constant prayer that the things that you learn and receive at your home church, and throughout your life, are the same things that you learn and receive at a Higher Things conference, and God-willing, it will also be what you in turn pass on to the next generation.

We are grateful to God to have been able to provide these conferences to give many the chance to get away to a solitary place as even our Lord often went to the mountains for a time to pray (Luke 5:16). However, we have offered these conferences over the years, not so that you could seek a mountain-top experience, but as a time to refresh yourselves with the higher things of God so that you can refocus around, and recalibrate with and through, what matters most.

The beauty of Higher Things is that while conference themes and their various foci may come and go, they ultimately emphasize the same exact thing. Every. Single. Time. God's Word doesn't change, but with each conference, with each turn of the diamond of God's Word, if you will, you see the same Word of God from a new and fresh perspective.

After 25 years of hosting conferences, Higher Things has developed almost a lectionary of conferences on various topics and themes, all of which reinforce and confess these same higher things. Just as with a lection, this book's task is to introduce those topics and themes to you once again.

Higher Things—the organization—is many things, but it is primarily about exactly what its name says—higher things. May it ever be so, not for the sake of Higher Things, but for the sake of the name of our savior, JESUS, who is the source, the content, and the identity of all things from above!

After all, what's in a name? Everything.

DYING TO LIVE

Higher Things: A Grandpa's Perspective

Rev. Harold Senkbeil

Looking Back

It's now just over a quarter century since my wife, Jane, and I spent four days with 700 others at the University of Wyoming in Laramie. Most of them were kids. Higher Things had just launched, and its founding leadership invited me to be a keynote speaker at the very first conference. It had been about six years since my *Dying to Live: The Power of Forgiveness* was published (CPH, 1994). In fact, they chose "Dying to Live" as the theme for that first conference. Plenary speakers tackled the major themes of the book; I provided brief, interspersed "color commentary" talks. The night before things kicked off, Jane and I unpacked a ton of books, and I inscribed one for each registered youth. Who knows? A few copies of that old first edition paperback with its funky purple and red cover containing my scrawled signature could be floating around in somebody's attic!

But a lot changed in a quarter century. That book went through several consecutive printings and at least one updated cover. Just recently, it came out in a newly revised second edition with long overdue updates[1]. Those fresh-faced teens who gathered in Laramie at the turn of the century are middle-aged now, many with children of their own. Most likely, some who shared those four days of fun, learning, and worship have gone on to higher things in eternal glory–like my wife. Jane died in December 2021, just after we celebrated our golden wedding anniversary. And as you can imagine, I'm not what I was at Laramie either. Back then, I was just a dad; now I'm a granddad. I have lots more grey hair (white, to be honest) than I did then. I now use a walking stick after foot surgery two years ago. Back then, I was a parish pastor; that, too, has changed considerably over twenty-five years. First, I helped train future pastors for six years,[2] then encouraged practicing pastors at conference retreats held all around the country and on three foreign continents for just over a decade.[3] But all that's behind me now. I've turned over the active pastoring and teaching to others younger and more able than I am.

Now What?

So where does that leave us now? It's clear that things are not what they once were. But then they never are. That's the way it is this side of eternity. Time has a way of pressing on toward the future. Years ago, as I stood at that podium in Laramie, looking into the faces of all those kids, I felt they were my window into the future. It was humbling to be there to pass along words of encouragement and faith to people I knew would be the moms and dads—grandmas and grandpas, even—of generations stretching far into the new millennium that began just months before. That's the way it's supposed to be,

---

[1] *Dying to Live: The Foundation, Focus, and Shape of the Christian Life* (CPH, 2025).

[2] Assoc Prof of Pastoral Ministry and Missions, Concordia Theological Seminary, Fort Wayne, Indiana, 2002-2008.

[3] Executive Director for Spiritual Care, DOXOLOGY: The Lutheran Center for Spiritual Care and Counsel, 2008-2019.

you know. Making disciples is a generational thing. By God's design, those who receive His infinite grace in His beloved Son are tasked with faithfully passing His abiding Word on to those who come after them (Deuteronomy 6:6-9).

A Lively Heritage

That's where tradition comes in. Tradition does not mean clinging to dry and meaningless customs, but literally, it means "hanging on" to the doctrine we've received from those who've gone before us and then "handing over" that living treasure to those who follow us.

- "Follow the pattern of the sound words that you have heard from me, in the faith and love that are in Christ Jesus. By the Holy Spirit who dwells within us, guard the good deposit entrusted to you" (2 Timothy 1:13-14).
- "...what you have heard from me in the presence of many witnesses entrust to faithful men, who will be able to teach others also" (2 Timothy 2:2).

Believe it or not, I once was a teenager. Back in the 1960s I was elected to leadership in something called "The Walther League." You can probably look it up online. It was a network of LCMS youth groups organized locally, regionally, and nationwide. Our country in those days was in turmoil. Racial tensions and war protests cropped up everywhere. Changing sexual standards challenged Christian life and faith. I'm an old man now, but the world kids face today is a lot like the world we faced back then. The more things change, the more they stay the same. Each generation faces peculiarly unique challenges to Christian life and faith. But in a way, they're actually only variations on one unchanging theme: People always prefer their way to God's way. Their own way leads through life to death. But although God's way is the way of the cross, it leads right through death into life in all its fullness.

So now it's your turn. Hang on to what you've learned, for sure. Take the time to read, mark, learn, and inwardly digest God's inspired Word. Ponder it deeply. Let its teachings sink deeply into your heart and soul. Then by the power of His Holy Spirit, let it shape your whole life—what you do with your body and what you think with your mind. Live your life inside out, for you are not your own. You were bought with a price—the holy, precious blood of Christ and his innocent suffering and death. You no longer live; for you died when you were baptized, and now you live in Jesus—and He lives in you (Galatians 2:20). When you were baptized, you were buried with him into his death and raised with him into his never-ending life. "So you also must consider yourselves dead to sin and alive to God in Christ Jesus" (Romans 6:1-11).

Pay It Forward

That's the ticket. That's the way you can move forward with hope and confidence in a world that seems to grow crazier every year. So whether you're a parent, a pastor, or just a kid, that's what I want to leave with you. I'm on my way out now; I've run my laps in the ongoing relay race, facing each and every generation. When it's our turn, we each need to get out of our comfort zones, step up, and have a go at it. Grab the baton of faith ever more tightly, run your race faithfully with all the energy God supplies you so generously, then carefully but firmly pass it along to those who come after you. In this endeavor, the race is not to the swift nor the battle to the strong (Ecclesiastes 9:11), but to those whose life is hidden with Christ in God (Colossians 3:3). He will supply all you need if you cling faithfully to Him by means of His sure Word and Holy Sacraments. Let your motto be that of Paul the Apostle: "I have been crucified with Christ. It is no longer I who live, but Christ who lives in me. And the life I now live in the flesh I live by faith in the Son of God, who loved me and gave himself for me (Galatians 2:20).

So hang in there. The world you're living in right now isn't all that different from the one the first Christians lived in. We're living in a chaotic world that's lost its Christian veneer; they lived in a tumultuous world that had no Christian vision at all. Their world was largely pagan; in many ways, ours grows increasingly pagan with every passing year. But that's no reason to despair. You and I have the same living Lord they did. With firm faith and unconquerable hope, they demonstrated to a watching world just what it really meant to live in Christ by dying to self. Then, by His Word, the Holy Spirit called their pagan neighbors to faith and gathered them into his church, where they were enlightened with his Gifts of forgiveness, life, and salvation. So the church in apostolic times lived and thrived no matter the threats on every side. You can read all about it in the Book of Acts.[4]

You're in Good Hands

So I'm not worried. Okay, I'm a little concerned. That's what grandpas do; they pray for their kids and their grandkids—and they fret a bit now and then. But I do know that God will see you through. You can't accomplish the mission all by yourself using your own resources, but he will equip you with everything you need if you remain faithful to him. "And I am sure of this, that he who began a good work in you will bring it to completion at the day of Jesus Christ" (Philippians 1:6).

I leave you with something I wrote for those kids back in 2000. Some of them may be your parents, for all I know. These lines of verse were inspired by the prayers and hymns we sang in evening prayer offices and at the Divine Service in Laramie. May they bring you courage, hope, and resolve to live each day for him who once was dead but now lives for you forever.

A Song in the Night

You shall have a song as in the night when a holy feast is kept;
And gladness of heart,
As when one sets out to the sound of the flute
To go to the mountain of the LORD, to the Rock of Israel.
And the LORD will cause His majestic voice to be heard....
[Isaiah 30:29-30, RSV]

---

[4] For an overview of the Book of Acts as a template for mission see Harold Senkbeil and Lucas Woodford, *The Culture of the Word: Faithful Ministry in a Post-Christian Society* (Lexham Press, 2026).

The organ muses in the night
Soft and deep it ponders mysteries profound
Calling all the faithful weary to the church's evening prayer:
    Seek *rest in Him who is your rest;*
    Find Light eternal midst gathering gloom of night

one flame sheds light into the dark
one voice pierces silent shadows of the night
then echoing, the church responds:
    Jesus Christ is the Light of the World
    The Light no darkness can overcome.
    Stay with us, Lord, for it is evening
    And the day is almost over

Gaining courage, young mouths find voice
Within the church's song
for unsung yearnings of the heart
    Kyrie eleison
    Lord, have mercy

You are worthy of being praised
With pure voices forever.

But where find that purity?
How cleanse the mouth
And purify the sinful heart and hands?
How drive deep despair from out this house of gloom and death?

Contrite hearts and broken spirits join
To speak the truth before the throne of God
    I, a poor, miserable sinner, confess...

Ears of faith hear the very words of Him who once was dead
But lives and holds the keys of death and hell
The Word of Life for sinners locked in prison cells of sin and shame
Forgiveness here on earth by Christ's very own command and will
    I forgive you all your sins in the Name
    of Father, Son, and Holy Spirit

Then the great Good Shepherd stoops down low to feed His dying flock
Under earthly bread and wine His very Body and true Blood
His living flesh and blood given once upon His cross
But now on earth the church's bread of heaven and wine of Joy
This Feast of Life a foretaste of the Feast still yet to come
Mouths open up to receive the very Life
That first was with the Father from all eternity
then took frail human flesh and blood within a virgin's womb

The Song of the Lamb and of His eternal bride the church
Echoes loud and long again on earth
and hearts are brave again, and arms are strong
He leads his people forth in joy
With shouts of thanksgiving

Old men and young men together
Sons and daughters—all one body, they
Menservants and maidservants join here on earth
To sing the church's ceaseless heavenly song
With one mouth giving glory here below
to Him who sits there above upon His throne
and to the Lamb once slain to lead forth Life from death

One Spirit and one Body
One Baptism and one Lord,
One God and Father of them all
One generation lauds His works to yet one more
The LORD's own voice is heard again on earth
His never-ending song is learned anew

So through the church the song goes unbroken on
That in these gray and latter days
There still are those whose life is praise
Each life a high doxology
Unto the Holy Trinity

Amen, Lord Jesus, quickly come
Let your light scatter the darkness
And illumine your church

Making Waves

How Can Water Do Such Great Things?

Rev. Peter Bender

"I am baptized!" Jesus wants you to know His love and have the certainty of salvation. Nothing is more important than to believe you are joined to Christ. "I am baptized!" Jesus has joined me to His death and resurrection! Jesus has clothed me with His righteousness! Jesus has forgiven me all my sin! I belong to Jesus Christ, the Son of God, my Savior! By this assurance, He comforts your conscience, protects you from Satan's accusations, gives you strength to live as His child, and restores to you the joy of His salvation. What He does for you in Holy Baptism, He does for every Christian in every land and every nation on earth. By Holy Baptism, we are joined to Christ, and we are united in a holy fellowship with one another in the forgiveness of sins.

The Small Catechism asks the simple, yet profound question, "How can water do such great things?" Answer: "Certainly not just water, but the word of God in and with the water does these things…" (Small Catechism).

Consider how God joined His Word and Spirit to water since the beginning of creation. The Spirit of God was hovering over the face of the waters. The Triune God of love created an expanse in the midst of the waters, dividing the water in the atmosphere from the water in the seas, rivers, and lakes. The dry land appeared, and He brought forth vegetation of every kind, created, sustained, and nourished by water and His Word. "Let there be ... and it was so!" He created the fish and creatures of the sea that move about the waters, and He created every animal that flies in the air or walks upon the earth. All living things are created and sustained by water and the Word of God. Take away water, and every living thing will die and be reduced to dust. But "how can water do such great things? Certainly not just water, but the Word of God in and with the water does these things."

The Lord God formed man of the dust of the ground, dry, lifeless dust, and breathed into His nostrils the breath of life, and Adam became a living being, fully alive, body and soul, hydrated by the Word and Spirit of God. By the breath of God, His Holy Spirit, man became alive! No wonder the church has confessed for centuries that the Holy Spirit is "the Lord and giver of life" (Nicene Creed). From the beginning of creation, the Holy Spirit created and sustained life by water and the Word. Before the Fall, a mist went up from the land, and a river flowed through Eden to become four riverheads to water the earth for the nourishment of life. The river that flowed out of Paradise pointed forward to the river of the water of life that gives salvation to all for the healing of the nations.

> The angel showed me the river of the water of life, bright as crystal, flowing from the throne of God and of the Lamb through the middle of the street of the city; also, on either side of the river, the Tree of Life with its twelve kinds of fruit, yielding its fruit each month. The leaves of the tree were for the healing of the nations. No longer will there be anything accursed, but the throne of God and of the Lamb will be in it, and his servants will worship him. (Revelation 22:1-3)

Here in the Book of Revelation, we see the connection between the water of life at creation and the water of life that Jesus gives in Holy Baptism. He is the source of forgiveness, life, and salvation, which flows to all nations through water. No wonder the psalmist declares, "There is a river whose streams make glad the city of God…" (Psalm 46:4), and Jesus says, "Whoever drinks of the water that I will give him will never be thirsty again. The water that I will give him will become in him a spring of water welling up to eternal life" (John 4:14).

The Old Testament connections to Holy Baptism continue. Noah was instructed by God's Word to build the ark. By the Word of God, the nations were called to repentance. By the Word of the Lord, the great deep was opened up, and the windows of heaven rained down water for forty days and forty nights. The Flood became the water of judgment for the impenitent, and the water of salvation for Noah and his family. The Flood was real water combined with God's Word. Without the water, there was no divine judgment! Without the water, there was no divine salvation! But with the Word of God, the Flood became "a life-giving water, rich in grace," through which all of creation was reborn, the Gift of salvation was given to Noah, and a new humanity sprang forth out of the water. This is why the Apostle Peter says, "Baptism now saves you!" (1 Peter 3:15). For, by the Word of God, Christ and the Gift of salvation for all nations are joined to the water. "For Christ also suffered once for sins, the righteous for the unrighteous, that he might bring us to God, being put to death in the flesh but made alive in the spirit, in which he went and proclaimed to the spirits in prison, because they formerly did not obey, when God's patience waited in the days of Noah, while the ark was being prepared, in which a few, that is, eight persons, were brought safely through water. Baptism, which corresponds to this, now saves you … through the resurrection of Jesus Christ, who has gone into heaven and is at the right hand of God" (1 Peter 3:18-22).

By the blood of the Passover Lamb, the children of Israel were redeemed from slavery in Egypt and brought to the shores of the Red Sea. Cliffs walling them in on either side, the Egyptian army pursuing them from behind, and the water of the sea lying before them, they had nowhere to go! In that moment, they were overwhelmed by sin, doubt, and unbelief. They had no strength to believe in the Lord or come to Him! But by the Word of the Lord, He came to them and saved them! It was a Word of pure grace! It was the gospel! "Fear not, stand firm, and see the salvation of the LORD, which he will work for you today ... The LORD will fight for you..." And by His Word, the waters of the Red Sea were parted, and the children of Israel passed through the waters on dry ground. It was real water! And by water and the Word, He saved them. This is what Christ accomplished for you in your Baptism. By the name of the Triune God—Father, Son, and Holy Spirit—in Baptism, you are joined to Christ, our Passover Lamb, whose blood sets you free from bondage to sin and rescues you from every accusation of the Evil One. It is as if He said to you in the midst of your helplessness, troubled conscience, and struggle to believe, "Do not be afraid! Stand still and see the salvation of the Lord! I will fight for you! You belong to Me! I will draw you through the water and bring you to safety!" By your Baptism into Christ, He has become your Lord, and you belong to Him. "How can water do such great things? Certainly not just water, but the Word of God in and with the water does these things!"

Then there was a leper named Naaman from the nation of Syria. He was the commander of the Syrian army. He was a mighty man of valor. He was full of self-righteousness and pride. He was impenitent. He believed that his money, wealth, and position could purchase his salvation and cleanse him of his leprosy. He had no faith in the Lord. He could not "by his own reason or strength believe in Jesus Christ, or come to Him" (Small Catechism, Third Article). But the Lord came to him through a seemingly nonsensical word of foolishness: "Go and wash in the Jordan seven times, and your flesh shall be restored, and you shall be clean" (2 Kings 5:10, 12). But Naaman resisted, "Are not the rivers of Damascus far superior to the muddy Jordan?" But by the Word of the Lord brought to him repeatedly by lowly messengers—a slave girl from Israel, a servant to the Prophet Elisha, and Naaman's own underlings—he was finally brought to repentance. His self-righteousness was crushed, and he was humbled. He washed in the Jordan according to the Word of God, and his flesh was restored like the flesh of a little child. Had Naaman turned away from the waters of the Jordan, he never would have been healed. But those waters, combined with God's Word, cleansed him. This Baptism in the Jordan River brought far more than physical healing to Naaman; it brought to him the Gift of salvation and complete cleansing from all his sin.

"How can water do such great things? Certainly not just water, but the Word of God in and with the water does these things" (Small Catechism). Holy Baptism saves because Jesus is the content of Baptism. When the Small Catechism says, "Baptism works forgiveness of sins, rescues from death and the devil, and gives eternal salvation to all who believe," it says this precisely because Jesus' death and resurrection are the content of Baptism. Consider these promises from the New Testament concerning the power and Gift of Baptism: "Whoever believes [in Christ] and is baptized will be saved..." (Mark 16:16); "Do you not know that all of us who have been baptized into Christ Jesus were baptized into his death? We were buried therefore with him by baptism into death, in order that, just as Christ was raised from the dead by the glory of the Father, we too might walk in newness of life..." (Romans 6:3-4); "For as many of you as were baptized into Christ have put on Christ..." (Galatians 3:27); "Baptism now saves you..." (1 Peter 3:15); "Repent and be baptized every one of you in the name of Jesus Christ for the forgiveness of your sins, and you will receive the gift of the Holy Spirit. For the promise [of baptism] is for you and for your children and for all who are far off, everyone whom the Lord our God calls to Himself..." (Acts 2:38-39); "Rise and be baptized and wash away your sins, calling on his name..." (Acts 22:16); "He saved us through the washing of rebirth and renewal by the Holy Spirit, whom He poured out on us generously through Jesus Christ our Savior, so that, having been justified by His grace, we might become heirs having the hope of eternal life. This is a trustworthy saying." (Titus 2:5-8a/Small Catechism). Baptism saves because Jesus' death and resurrection for the forgiveness of sins is the very content of Holy Baptism. Baptism saves because Jesus saves!

But what role does faith play? Faith receives what the Word gives. The Word of God gives Jesus into the water of Baptism. The Word of God gives to Baptism its power to forgive sins, to rescue from death and the devil, and to give eternal salvation for Jesus' sake. Faith receives what the Word gives, and the Word always gives us Jesus, and by the Word of God, Jesus is joined to the water. So the Small Catechism rightly confesses how the benefits of Baptism are given: "Certainly not just water, but the word of God in and with the water does these things, ***along with the faith*** [emphasis added] which trusts this word of God in the water." What role, therefore, does faith play? Answer: It trusts the Word of God in the water. We see this in Naaman, who, by the Word of God, was brought to repentance and faith to receive the benefits of this washing in the Jordan River. By virtue of the Word of God, neither the Word nor the washing in the water could be omitted. Naaman would not have been cleansed unless he believed that the Word of promise attached to the water, and being called to faith by the Word of promise, he entered the Jordan to be cleansed. Unbelief rejects Christ; faith receives Him. Unbelief rejects Baptism; faith receives Baptism. Yet even this faith is a miracle and Gift of the Holy Spirit through the Word. This, too, is of great comfort for you! All depends upon His Word! "Faith comes from hearing, and hearing through the word of Christ" (Romans 10:17). "Faith ... is not your own doing; it is the gift of God, not a result of works, so that no one may boast" (Ephesians 2:8b-9). So the Small Catechism concludes, "For without God's word the water is plain water and no baptism. But with the Word of God, it is a baptism, that is, a life-giving water, rich in grace, and a washing of the new birth in Holy Spirit, as St. Paul says in Titus chapter three."

Since all nations descended from the one man Adam and since all are redeemed from sin, death, and the power of the devil by the Second Adam, our Lord Jesus Christ, no wonder Jesus declared to His Church, in the last chapter of Matthew, "Therefore go and make disciples of all nations, baptizing them in the name of the Father and of the Son and of the Holy Spirit" (Matthew 28:19). Baptism speaks of God's universal grace for all mankind. Baptism is central to how God makes disciples of all nations. By water and the Word, the Gift of salvation is extended to every nation and tribe of people. So "baptism is not just plain water, but it is the water included in God's command:" *Go and make disciples of all nations* ... "and combined with God's word:" *baptizing them in the name of the Father and of the Son and of the Holy Spirit* (Small Catechism).

It is in Jesus' Baptism that we see the mystery and miracle of the Holy Trinity in our Baptism. John the Baptist had been calling sinners to repentance and baptizing them for the forgiveness of sins with the promise that they would receive the Spirit from Him whose way he was preparing. The people of Jerusalem, Judea, and all around the Jordan heard John's call and came to him for Baptism, confessing their sin. When Jesus appeared before John to be baptized, John was confused. "I have need to be baptized by You, and are You coming to me?" (Matthew 3:14). It is as if John were saying, "I am the sinner. You are the sinless One. Why do You need to be baptized? You have no sin! You need no forgiveness!" But Jesus catechizes John on the wondrous miracle of Baptism, saying, "Let it be so now, for thus it is fitting for us to fulfill all righteousness." How does Jesus' Baptism fulfill all righteousness? Jesus entered into the Jordan River, not to have His sins forgiven, but to take our sins upon Himself! In Holy Baptism, Jesus aligns Himself with us and takes upon Himself the sin of the whole world. The Apostle Paul declares of Jesus, "God made Him who knew no sin, to be sin for us, that we might become the righteousness of God in Him!" (2 Corinthians 5:21 NKJV). This is precisely the miracle of our Baptism. It is, as Luther said, a blessed and happy exchange! Your sin is laid upon Jesus. He sheds His blood and dies for you upon the cross. By His death, the condemnation of the Law is taken away, and forgiveness is won for you, and not for you only, but also for the sins of the whole world. The forgiveness of sins that Jesus won for you in His death is what raises Jesus from the dead, and because you are joined to Him in Baptism, His forgiveness raises you from the dead! "All of us who have been baptized into Christ Jesus were baptized into his death. ... Just as Christ was raised from the dead by the glory of the Father, we too might walk in newness of life" (Romans 6:3-4). In your Baptism, you receive the righteousness of Christ as your very own! "As many of you as were baptized into Christ have put on Christ!" (Galatians 3:27). "I am baptized!" Therefore, I belong to Christ, and He belongs to me!

It is in Jesus' Baptism that you see the miracle of the Holy Trinity in your own Baptism. You were baptized in the name of the Father and of the Son and of the Holy Spirit. Each of the three persons of the Holy Trinity is present for your salvation in the water of your Baptism. For Jesus' sake, **God the Father** speaks from heaven, "You are My beloved, in whom I am well pleased!" **The Son** is the very content of the water of your Baptism. He is your righteousness! You are baptized into Christ, the beloved Son of the Father, who has fulfilled the whole will and Law of God for you, so that whether you are male or female, Jew or Gentile, slave or free, you are given the status of sonship—the very sonship of Christ Himself—for you belong to Him (Galatians 3:27-29). That is your baptismal identity! Finally, as **the Holy Spirit** descended upon Jesus in His Baptism in the form of a dove, that great symbol of peace, so the Holy Spirit descended upon you in Baptism for the Gift of faith in Christ and peace with God the Father, through the forgiveness of sins in Jesus' name. You became a temple of the Holy Spirit. Christ dwells in you by the ministry of His Word and Sacraments. Your Baptism gives you the right to pray, and it gives you the promise of the Holy Spirit whenever you hear the Word and receive Christ's Absolution.

The divine name—Father, Son, and Holy Spirit—is the Word of God "combined" with the water in Holy Baptism. But this divine name is not a magic formula. It is not hocus pocus. It has meaning. Each of the three persons of the Trinity is actually active in the Baptism of every Christian. The Apostle Paul opens up for us the significance of the divine name in the baptismal formula and how each person of the Trinity is involved. It is a citation from Titus chapter 3, quoted in the Small Catechism under the question, "How can water do such great things?" By explicitly supplying the names of each person of the Holy Trinity to this passage, it becomes easier to see the operation of each of the persons of the Trinity in the baptismal formula, "I baptize you in the name of the Father and of the Son and of the Holy Spirit." Paul writes, "He [God **the Father**] saved us through the washing of rebirth and renewal by **the Holy Spirit** [Holy Baptism], whom He [God **the Father**] poured out on us generously through Jesus Christ our Savior [**the Son**], so that, having been justified by His [God **the Father's**] grace, we might become heirs [with **the Son**] having the hope of eternal life. This is a trustworthy saying" (Titus 3:5b-8a). This passage is rich! God the Father saved you by grace and justified you in His Son. God the Father gave you, through His Son, a washing that rebirthed and renewed you by His Holy Spirit, who was poured out upon you in the water of Baptism. You are an heir with His Son and have the sure and certain hope of eternal life in Jesus.

What God gave you in your Baptism, God desires to give to everyone from every nation under heaven. By the preaching of His Word and the ministry of His Holy Spirit, God is making waves among all nations. In the great commission, Jesus said, "Go and make disciples ... baptizing them...and teaching them." In God's way of making disciples, Baptism and catechesis go together. This teaching, which we call catechesis, is not merely the communication of knowledge or information; it is the very way in which God encounters us through His Word, calling us to repentance and declaring us righteous for Jesus' sake. In catechesis, God speaks to us, and we speak back to Him in faith, confessing our sins, claiming His promises, and crying out to Him for the strength to be faithful disciples of Jesus. Catechesis is God's unique way of teaching, which converts sinners to the new life of faith in Christ for the forgiveness of sins. From this miracle of faith in Christ, Jesus' forgiveness and mercy teach and empower us to live in Christ's love in service to others. God's way of teaching turns us all into little children. This is why Jesus said, "Whoever does not receive the kingdom of God as a little child will by no means enter it" (Mark 10:15). So Jesus told Nicodemus, "You must be born from above!" (John 3:7). We all must become little children before God.

But how does this happen? How do mature adults become little children? What does it mean to be "a little child" before God? Look at a little child, an infant, a helpless baby. He is completely dependent upon his mother. He can't feed himself. He can't diaper himself. He can't dress himself. He needs his mother's loving care for everything he needs. She not only gave birth to him, but she also feeds him, changes his diaper, and dresses him. She teaches him by her loving words and actions to trust and to love. Is this not what the church does for us and for sinners of all nations who are adopted into the family of God? Is not the church the very bride of Christ and the mother of the children of God? The children of God are conceived, born, and nurtured by water and the Word. The Word is not only attached to the water; the Word is also how she nurtures her children. She brings children of God into the world, from all nations, through the new birth of Baptism and the nurturing love of catechesis. Those who become as little children are those who have been brought to contrition. They have been brought to repentance. They have been turned from self-reliance to dependence upon Jesus, from self-righteousness to faith in Christ's righteousness as their very own. This is what catechesis is all about. A "little child" of God confesses, "I'm a sinner! I cannot save myself! But Christ is my righteousness! He has saved me! I belong to Him!" The faith we received at our Baptism is nurtured throughout our lives by this catechesis, so that we remain totally dependent on Jesus. As little children, catechesis teaches us how to confess our sins, how to forgive one another, how to receive forgiveness, how to pray, and how to live where God has called us with faith in Jesus and love for others. By Holy Baptism, we are born into this family, and by catechesis, we learn to live the baptismal life and share this life with others.

Learn by heart the Small Catechism. It gives you the content of the baptismal life and "the pattern of sound words" (2 Timothy 1:13) by which we live the Christian life and pass on the faith to the next generation of Christians from all nations.

The Ten Commandments are God's Law. The Ten Commandments not only teach us what is good and right, what it means to love God and our neighbor, but they also show us our sin and how much we need our Savior. God's Law is necessary in the preaching of repentance. Self-righteousness and pride must be crushed. The sinful nature must be put to death. Every sinner must be called to see their sin as rebellion against God for which they deserve God's wrath. Only then can we receive Christ and what He has done for us upon the cross. Only then will we be led back to the promises of our Baptism in daily contrition and repentance: "I am a baptized child of God! Lord, forgive me, help me, strengthen me to be faithful. I ask for Your grace. I want to do better." We learn by heart the Ten Commandments that we might be led to Jesus every day of our lives because He has fulfilled the Law for us. This baptismal pattern of daily dying and rising with Christ in contrition and repentance continues throughout the lifetime of a baptized child of God.

The Creed proclaims the Gospel of God's love in Christ. It is in the Creed that we see the work of the Holy Trinity, Father, Son, and Holy Spirit, into whose name we are baptized for the forgiveness of sins. At the heart of the Creed is God's undeserved love and mercy and the confession of a baptized child of God: "Jesus Christ is my Lord, who has redeemed me, a lost and condemned person, purchased and won me from all sin, from death, and from the power of the devil, not with gold or silver, but with His holy precious blood and with His innocent suffering and death, that I may be His own" (Second Article). "That I may be His own!" There is great comfort and strength for you in this confession. "I am baptized! I do not belong to the devil! I belong to Christ! He is my Lord! He is my righteousness! His forgiveness covers me, protects me, and strengthens me to be His child!" The Ten Commandments show us our sin, but the Creed proclaims the love of God in Christ and the faith to which every baptized child of God clings.

The Lord's Prayer is the prayer of the baptized children of God. Because we are joined to the Father's Son in Baptism, we are bold to call upon God as "our Father." The Lord's Prayer is Jesus' gift to us. As baptized children of God, we have confidence to approach our heavenly Father, for Jesus' sake, claiming every promise He has made to us. "I am baptized into Christ!" This is the holy life of a Christian—a life that is marked by faith in Christ and confident prayer as the voice of faith. As children of God, we have free and open access to the Father for Jesus' sake, just as little children run to their parents for help and comfort in every need. With the words, "Our Father who art in heaven … God tenderly invites us to believe that He is our true Father and that we are His true children, so that with all boldness and confidence we may ask Him as dear children ask their dear Father" (Lord's Prayer).

The next three parts of the Catechism, together with the Table of Duties and Daily Prayers, teach us how, as the children of God, our faith in Christ is created, nourished, and expressed in our daily lives. **The Sacrament of Holy Baptism** regenerates sinners and makes us Christians. It unites us with the death and resurrection of Jesus Christ for the forgiveness of sins and bestows upon us the Gift of the Holy Spirit and faith in Christ. It gives us the rights and privileges of the children of God who are joint heirs with Christ of all the treasures of heaven. **Confession and Absolution** return us to the promises of our Baptism daily. Jesus' forgiveness, received from our pastors and shared with one another in the family of God, strengthens our faith in Christ, reconciles brothers and sisters with one another, and gives us comfort and help against sin and temptation. **The Sacrament of the Altar** is the very Body and Blood of Christ for salvation. It is the medicine against our sinful flesh, the sin and trouble of this world, and the temptations of the devil. It is the celebration of the Lord's forgiveness that is mutually shared with one another within the body of Christ. The Lord's Supper is given that we might learn to believe that Christ, out of great love, died for our sin, so that we also learn from Him to love God and one another. It is from the preaching of the Gospel of Jesus' forgiveness and the reception of the Lord's Supper that we, as the children of God, live in our station and calling in life as described in **the Table of Duties.** In this baptismal life, we pray with confidence the Catechism's **Daily Prayers,** which begin and end each day with the sign of the Holy Cross "in the name of the Father and of the Son and of the Holy Spirit."

Every day of your life, when you rise up in the morning to a new day, say to yourself, "I am baptized! I belong to Christ! I am His and He is mine!" Life will be filled with challenges, disappointments, heartache, the struggle with sin, temptation, and Satan's accusations. But your Baptism will not fail you. Jesus walked on the water (Matthew 14:22-33). Every enemy—sin, death, the judgment of the Law, and the devil's power—is under His feet! In Jesus, they are all defeated, and the victory is won! Baptism gives you that victory. Through the water of Holy Baptism, Jesus is always saying to you, "Come to Me!" No matter what you face, no matter how far you may have fallen, He stands upon the water with outstretched arms saying, "Come to Me!" And if you, like Peter, should begin to sink and drown, it is Jesus who reaches out to you, raising you up from death to life. "I am baptized! Thanks be to God!"

In His Face

Rev. Grant Knepper

What does it mean to be in His face? This is an important question because in our time and place, getting in someone's face is usually used to describe confrontation. You get in someone's face when you are upset. You get in someone's face to tell them what they have done wrong. You get in someone's face when you are angry. You get in someone's face when they really deserve what is coming to them. Anger is only part of it; in addition, if you really want to get into someone's face, you must be present to do it properly. You simply cannot get into someone's face from a distance. When it comes to getting in someone's face, there is no app for that.

That is how it is with us. We like to show our anger in the most personal way possible. We don't want to be angry from a distance. We like to show our anger up close and personal. When we are angry, we want to be present enough that the other person knows it. We want them to be reminded of our anger and have no rest from our anger. We want to remain in their face.

The other side of this is that we do not like it when other people get in our faces. That kind of angry presence makes us uncomfortable.

No one wants to be around someone who is actively angry at them. Having someone in your face is no fun. Anger from family or friends who are in your face is bad enough; now imagine if it were God who was in your face. Imagine if God were angry enough with you to get in your face and let you know what you had done wrong and that you deserved what was coming to you. Imagine if when it came to God that being in His face was to be in the presence of an angry deity that could never be placated. This would make God's face something to be feared and avoided at all costs. The last thing you would want is to be in the presence of a God who was angry at you. You would want to be in any other place than in His face.

Thankfully, with God, things are not like this. His thoughts are not our thoughts, and His ways are not our ways. When it comes to the presence of God, when it comes to being *in His face,* things are different. God's presence is not a sign of his anger but of his love and approval. Those whom God is angry with are driven from his face; they are denied his presence. Look at the story of Cain and Abel in Genesis 4. After Cain murders Abel and God has pronounced his punishment, "Cain said to the LORD, 'My punishment is greater than I can bear. Behold, you have driven me today away from the ground, and from your face I shall be hidden'" (Genesis 4:13-14). Cain had sinned. Cain was in the wrong. Cain deserved what was coming to him, and the result was that Cain lost his place in God's face. Cain lost his place in the presence of God. Luther put Cain's predicament this way: "Cain went out and came to another place. Here there was no face of God and no visible sign by which he could comfort himself that God was with him and was favorably inclined toward him."[1]

The implication here is that to be in His face is to be in a place of comfort and security, to be in a place where you know that God Himself is for you. The Book of Psalms is filled with language that shows being in His face was something that was sought after by God's people. In Psalm 4, David says, "There are many who say, 'Who will show us some good? Lift up the light of your face upon us, O LORD!'

---

[1] Martin Luther, *Luther's Works, Vol. 1: Lectures on Genesis: Chapters 1-5*, ed. Jaroslav Jan Pelikan, Hilton C. Oswald, and Helmut T. Lehmann, vol. 1 (Saint Louis: Concordia Publishing House, 1999), 309.

You have put more joy in my heart than they have when their grain and wine abound. In peace I will both lie down and sleep; for you alone, O LORD, make me dwell in safety" (Psalm 4:6-8). Conversely, the language of lament is used when God's presence seems to be far away. David writes in Psalm 13, "How long, O LORD? Will you forget me forever? How long will you hide your face from me?" (Psalm 13:1). Similar language is used in the New Testament to describe what the full coming of God's kingdom will be like for His people. Paul writes, "For now we see in a mirror dimly, but then face to face. Now I know in part; then I shall know fully, even as I have been fully known" (1 Corinthians 13:12). while John tells us that in the Jerusalem come down from Heaven, "They will see his face, and his name will be on their foreheads" (Revelation 22:4).

Meanwhile, those who are not part of the people of God have no place in His kingdom, have no place in the heavenly Jerusalem, have no place in His face. "But as for the cowardly, the faithless, the detestable, as for murderers, the sexually immoral, sorcerers, idolaters, and all liars, their portion will be in the lake that burns with fire and sulfur, which is the second death" (Revelation 21:8). They, like Cain, will have no place of security or comfort because God will not be with them nor favorably inclined toward them.

This is where it gets interesting. At first glance, it appears that the Christian life can be reduced to doing those things that allow you to stay in His face while avoiding those things that would cause Him to remove you from His face. What those things are is no mystery. God's law is revealed in the Scriptures for all to see. The standard is clear. You are called to be holy because God is holy.

It turns out that it is not as simple as it sounds. The law makes demands but is of no help when it comes to meeting those demands. The law can demand holiness, but it cannot deliver holiness. In fact, it just shows you that you don't deserve a place in His face. As Paul writes in Romans, "For by works of the law no human being will be justified in his sight, since through the law comes knowledge of sin" (Romans 3:20).

If it were just up to the law, then you and everybody else would end up sharing the same fate as Cain. Cast out from God's face with no place of security and no visible sign that God was for you. Such is the fate of sinners under the law.

Thankfully, the law is not God's only word to you. The law is not your ticket into His face, nor is the law what allows you to stay in His face. Paul continues his thought in Romans 3 about the righteousness of God apart from the law (Romans 3:21). Luther puts it this way, "The knowledge of the Gospel is the face of God, the message that we have grace and truth through the death of Christ."[2] This means that to be in His face is to be caught up in the gospel. To be in His face is to partake of God's promises that were all fulfilled in Christ. To be in His face is to have a place of comfort and security and to know that God is for you even though you are a sinner.

You do not have to quest after the presence of God because God brought his presence to you. Jesus became incarnate; he took on flesh and entered into the fallen world. He brought the face of God into the world to save the world. Jesus brought you into His face by dying on the cross and rising from the dead. Jesus ended the reign of sin for all. Jesus ended the reign of sin for you.

This makes God's presence and your place in it His gift to you and not something that you earn. This makes being in His face something that is part of your life, even now as you live as a fallen being in a fallen world. What awaits you in the full coming of God's kingdom at the end has already broken into your everyday life in the here and now.

Here is the truth of your Baptism. In the waters of the font, you entered into His face, and He called you by name, claimed you as His own, and made you one of His people. What Christ did on the cross for all was applied to you personally; there, the righteousness of God that is apart from the law was given to you. While this is an event that is in your past, it is an event that you can return to daily as you remember your Baptism. When the law is having its way with you, when you are faced with temptation, when Satan himself is attacking you, you can take comfort in your Baptism and know for sure that God is for you and that you remain in His face.

The same is true each time you participate in the Divine Service. Every time you go to church, you are in His face. Every time your

---

[2] Martin Luther, *Luther's Works, Vol. 22: Sermons on the Gospel of St. John: Chapters 1-4*, ed. Jaroslav Jan Pelikan, Hilton C. Oswald, and Helmut T. Lehmann, vol. 22 (Saint Louis: Concordia Publishing House, 1999), 158.

pastor begins a service with the invocation, "In the name of the Father, and of the Son, and of the Holy Spirit," it serves as a reminder of your Baptism. When you take part in Confession and Absolution, you are in His face to receive His forgiveness. In the word of forgiveness that comes from your pastor is the forgiveness of God, and another reminder that God is for you and that you are secure in His face. In the readings are the stories of God's people of ages past that lived in the same promises that you live in now. They, like you, are in His face. In the sermon is the proclamation of the gospel, and you hear again that what Christ did on the cross He did for you. In the prayer of the church, you can address God directly because you are there with Him. You know that your petitions are welcomed and heard because you are in His face.

The Divine Service reaches its climax in the sacrament of Communion, where you eat and drink the Body and Blood of the Lord for the strengthening of faith and the forgiveness of sins. In the very presence of God, you receive the Gifts of God. In His face, you receive all that you need for this life and the life to come. In the here and the now, you receive a foretaste of what is to come.

Even when you are not at church, He is with you, and you remain in His face. You carry Him with you wherever you go, and because He is with you, you can share him with others. Your place in His face is secure, but there is always room for more. What God did for you, He did for all people. Jesus is for all people, the cross is for all people, and the God who is for you is for all people. He desires that all people be in His face.

Rev. Harrison Goodman

Then I saw a new heaven and a new earth, for the first heaven and the first earth had passed away, and the sea was no more. And I saw the holy city, new Jerusalem, coming down out of heaven from God, prepared as a bride adorned for her husband. And I heard a loud voice from the throne saying, "Behold, the dwelling place of God is with man. He will dwell with them, and they will be his people, and God himself will be with them as their God. He will wipe away every tear from their eyes, and death shall be no more, neither shall there be mourning, nor crying, nor pain anymore, for the former things have passed away."
—Revelation 21:1-4

John sees the city of God in a vision. Part of the new heavens and new earth, it is a blessed picture of the Church Triumphant. These are the ones brought out of the great tribulation, their robes washed white in the blood of the Lamb. The old has passed away. The new has come. They sing their alleluias because they are near Jesus (Revelation 7). On this side of glory, we sing them in joyful expectation. For us, the words "first heaven and first earth" are loaded with enough misery that everyone's glad to see them pass away. With them go sin, death, and the power of the devil. Each enemy comes undone in the victory of the crucified and risen God.

Outside the city are...people who sin like us. Liars. Cowards. Idolators. The sexually immoral. But your sin has come undone in the image of Revelation. You are the ones prepared as the bride of Christ, cleansed in the washing of water with the word, presented without blemish or spot (Ephesians 5). You didn't earn your place in the city. You are baptized into your citizenship. The devil is finally locked away in a lake of fire. You didn't conquer him, but he was conquered by the blood of the Lamb (Revelation 12). The victory of Eden is restored as God once again walks with His people, now not to promise what will be, but to be what was once promised. To Him, they are the same, bound up in His name. I AM. The sea will be no more, nor any of the death it brings. Jesus strode across the sea, walking over death itself. Jesus, who calms the storm, rescuing the disciples, puts away the source of death altogether at last. Sin. It is nailed to the cross and atoned for. Finished. You are the ones that Jesus died for, forgiven, holy, loved, and saved. The ones left out of the gates are those who would bar themselves from it and be known by something other than His mercy. Lord, have mercy.

I want to go to the city of God. I want to be away from the misery that wracks the church militant, those faithful who are yet striving against the enemies brought to nothing in the resurrection (Romans 6). It's a promise we're desperate enough to try and build. We wouldn't be the first. We've tried to build cities with towers that climb to the heavens. But Babel and her towers have never been the way to heaven. Building up over the bones of those who don't get to dwell at the top. The sinners not like us. The ones who could not keep up. The ones different enough to be cast down. Sinful minds, upon being told there will be people outside of heaven, make lists of who to fill it with and plan to climb up past them.

But the City of God is not what we build up to heaven. It descends, coming down from heaven from God. Because God comes down from heaven to save sinners, whether they sin like you or not. For God did not send his Son into the world to condemn the world, but in order that the world might be saved through him (John 3). And this, our

Lord descending to save, is how our church is built. For in saying, "He ascended," what does it mean but that he had also descended into the lower regions, the earth? He who descended is the one who also ascended far above all the heavens, that he might fill all things. And he gave the apostles, the prophets, the evangelists, the shepherds and teachers, to equip the saints for the work of ministry, for building up the body of Christ, until we all attain to the unity of the faith and of the knowledge of the Son of God, to mature manhood, to the measure of the stature of the fullness of Christ (Ephesians 4). It means the City of God is found this side of glory as a shelter for the church militant.

Psalm 46:4-7: There is a river whose streams make glad the city of God, the holy habitation of the Most High. God is in the midst of her; she shall not be moved; God will help her when morning dawns. The nations rage, the kingdoms totter; he utters his voice, the earth melts. The LORD of hosts is with us; the God of Jacob is our fortress. Selah

Because the dwelling place of God is with man. So when nations rage, and kingdoms totter, and it all feels like it's about to fall down, remember that the City of God is not a far-off hope but a present one. The kingdom is where the king has authority. And our King came down to earth to exercise His authority not chiefly in power but in mercy.

It gives words to Luther's most famous hymn, crafted around Psalm 46, "A Mighty Fortress." It's a hymn for the Church Militant. It's very honest about the state of the world. The devil prowls about. The world is against the truth. We imagine shelter in the City of God to be something free from sin, death, and the devil. Instead, it grants you freedom from them. God wields His authority in mercy, not just power. He saves the sinners. He dies for all the world. It's messy today, because rather than simply annihilating everything evil today, including you, He bears evil, patiently forgiving, until that last great day. Until then, He shields you, safeguards you, and grants you residence under Him. This leaves a place to find shelter, a citizenship that is yours on earth that ties you to heaven.

When Christians speak of heaven being our home, it isn't just that we're looking forward to getting out of this place. It's that we take shelter under Christ, because heaven is not a cloud where nothing bad happens. Heaven is wherever Jesus is. This is why Christ's first words in the Gospel of Mark point out that heaven has come to earth. The kingdom of God is at hand (Mark 1). This is why we sing with angels and archangels and all the company of heaven as our Lord is bodily present during the Sacrament of the Altar. Heaven isn't a bodiless place away from bad. Heaven is wherever Jesus is. And Jesus is incarnate, comes to earth, and saves you. Jesus is still present here for you in word and sacrament. This is where the church militant abides in the City of God. The thing that makes glad the city is the river, the water, the salvation that makes us unmovable from her. Your Baptism gives hope not only for a future, but for today as well.

Now, go back and look at the tenses. The Church Triumphant feels like a future tense for us, but we're a part of it now. Jesus is what joins together the Church Militant and the Church Triumphant. The church is the city of God because the dwelling place of God is with man. Militant and triumphant are only glances at moments in time, but she is made up of the same saints because she is saved by the same Christ.

Today you kneel in the church. It feels so deeply like war that we call ourselves the militant, even though the war is already won. Christ called it finished. So while the earth gives way, Christ is our mighty fortress. When we kneel in the church today, we are tied to the triumph of the last great day. Eden will be restored. This time it will be cultivated. No longer just a garden, we will inhabit a city. Babel will be reversed, crafted apart from a desire to escape earth and climb up; our Lord comes down to dwell with His people. Tears will be wiped away. Death comes undone once for all, and with it, every reason to ever weep again.

He is our bridegroom. We are His bride. He will not be far from us. Measure the City of God based on the Bridegroom's nearness, not whether or not it rains on the wedding day. Christ is near in word and sacrament. You dwell today in the City of God. You, today, are a saint. Tied to heaven. Tied to Jesus. Today, militant, but there is nothing that can separate you from His triumph.

Rev. Brett Simek

"Dare to be Lutheran" is more than a conference theme. It has served as a theme and unofficial mission statement for Higher Things for over twenty years and is even a trademarked phrase of Higher Things. It is such a core and foundational theme, used over and over again, that it has made this nonsensical jumble of letters, "DTBL," mean something: "Dare to be Lutheran."

But, if we are going to dare to be Lutheran, we must ask the Lutheran question about this theme: What does this mean? There are two fundamental parts to be broken down, explained, and addressed. First, why the word "Dare"? And second, why the word "Lutheran"? What does it mean to "Dare," and what does it mean to "be Lutheran"? These are the two important questions we must answer if we are going to understand what it means to "Dare to be Lutheran."

So, just as many good Lutheran churches fill their pews from the back to the front, we are going to start at the end and move to the beginning. What does it mean to be Lutheran? If you have a few spare minutes or hours, maybe even days, you should ask your pastor this question. There are books upon books filled with trying to explain this very thing. While I admit I haven't read them all, I will say that at the very heart, core, and foundation of all of them is the very same thing. The very heart and soul of what it is to be distinctly and uniquely Lutheran is found, not in Luther, but in Christ.

We may not be the only Christian denomination to say and claim that our center and focus is on Jesus Christ, but the way in which we view Him, believe in Him, teach Him, and confess Him is unique. That is not to say that no other Christian denominations can get into heaven, but that the Jesus we believe, teach, and confess delivers unique forgiveness, comfort, and peace. Or, to use a single term, we hold to a unique Gospel.

This proclamation of Jesus isn't unique in that we are the only ones ever to preach it. This Gospel didn't start with us, with Lutherans, or with Luther, but it is the same faith, the same Jesus, the same Gospel message that Jesus preached, that the apostles preached, that the early church fathers preached, and ancient churches preached. In fact, both the source and the object of the Lutheran faith are one and the same, Jesus.

The answer to what it means to "be Lutheran" is found in Jesus. It's all about Jesus. It's all about the Word made flesh. It's all about

> Jesus Christ, [the Father's] only Son, our Lord, who was conceived by the Holy Spirit, born of the Virgin Mary, suffered under Pontius Pilate, was crucified, died, and was buried. He descended into hell. The third day He rose again from the dead. He ascended into heaven and sits at the right hand of God the Father Almighty. From thence He will come to judge the living and the dead.

We believe exactly what the Apostles' Creed confesses and getting the "who" and the "what" of Jesus right is the first step.

Jesus is fully God and fully Man, begotten of the Father from eternity and born of Mary. God became Man to unite God and Man together. By His perfect life, He perfectly fulfilled the Law that we cannot fulfill on our behalf. By His sacrificial death upon the cross, He endured the judgment, wrath, and punishment of sin on our behalf. By His resurrection, He overcame sin, death, and the devil to be victorious with life everlasting on our behalf.

We could not do it for ourselves. We could not even begin or think to begin turn from sin no more than a dead person can think to raise them self from death for we are dead in our trespasses and sins (Ephesians 2:1). It is by God's unmotivated, undeserved grace alone, without any merit or worthiness in us, that Jesus Christ comes to stand in our place and be our salvation. This is what the Word of God, the Word made flesh, teaches and preaches to us: His Law and His Gospel. By His Word alone, by Scripture alone as the highest and greatest authority, holding both church tradition and our own reason and logic as servants to His Word, we have salvation.

The Word made flesh, revealed in the Word inspired and written in the Scriptures, are the teachings of the church called doctrine. Yet, this doctrine is not mere history nor abstract or idle thought—Lutheran doctrine is for you. It is all Jesus for you, on your behalf, on your side, doing enough for you, all that is necessary for you, for your forgiveness, for your salvation. We see this no better than in His Sacraments.

In the Sacraments of Baptism and the Lord's Supper, as well as in Confession, the historical Jesus who was born, baptized, crucified, and raised thousands of years ago meets us here, now, today. In these Gifts, God bridges the gap of time between us and Him so that we are united together. The Gifts from back then are delivered to us today.

In Baptism, we are united to Him through water and Word. Just as He was baptized, so are we baptized. We are baptized to wash away our sin and death, yet He is baptized to take it upon Himself. By God's Word, by the power of the Holy Spirit, our stories, our lives meet that Word made flesh as the water and Word are put upon us. Christ is put upon us (Galatians 3:27). His death and resurrection are put upon us (Romans 6:4). His forgiveness is put upon us. He is for us. By faith in these Words, He is made yours, and you are made His.

In the Lord's Supper, His Body and Blood, the very Body and Blood that hung upon the cross, are for you. The bread is His body, and the wine is His blood (Matthew 26:26-28). Take and eat. Take and drink. He has instituted, planned, and purposed this meal for the very purpose of uniting Himself to you. In this eating and drinking, we are made participants (1 Corinthians 10:16) and beneficiaries of His death and resurrection. The Word is for you to eat and drink for your forgiveness, life, and salvation. By faith in these Words, He is made yours, and you are made His.

This is the unique comfort of being distinctly Lutheran: Jesus, the Word made flesh, written, and proclaimed; Law and Gospel; grace alone, faith alone, Scripture alone; Word and Sacraments; for you and for your salvation. This doctrine and these teachings are enough. They are enough to create and sustain saving faith. They are enough for you. They are enough for the church. They are enough for the next generation. Yet this beautiful and comforting historic Lutheran doctrine and teachings, while enough by themselves, are not by themselves, it is not alone for doctrine informs and shapes practice.

Our practice of this Word, like our doctrine, is historic. Our worship is shared with those who have gone before us in the faith. It does not need to be a novelty or "eye-catching" because it is heart-changing. In it, God, the Father, Son, and Holy Spirit that we confess with the Apostles' and in that creed, is at work to create and sustain saving faith just as He has for generations who have come before us, He will continue to do for us and for generations that follow us.

In the Psalms, the reading and preaching of God's Word, distinguishing Law and Gospel, administering His Sacraments, God's saving work is done, His Word is delivered to bring us out of this darkness into His marvelous light. His Divine Service to us is enough as it consistently delivers Christ and His Gifts that we might serve Him with our thanks and praise.

Just like doctrine, the Word made flesh and written, distinguishing Law and Gospel, the Word and the Sacraments are not necessarily easy but require teaching for understanding, so, too, does the Divine Service. Yet this is a gift worth teaching, worth working to maintain, for in it are unique Gifts and protections.

The Divine Service, the liturgy and hymnody of the church connect us to Christ. They connect us to the body of Christ and to those who have gone before us. These things, these elements of service and worship, have been handed down to us as the greatest hits and best Gifts the church can give to pass down the faith which saves. Our liturgy and order of worship was not created overnight but has been shaped, molded, crafted carefully and intentionally by the greatest minds of the church and Her faithful servants with the sole purpose and intention of bringing that saving Word to you that you might believe, receive His Gifts, and have everlasting life in His kingdom.

Just like the liturgy, so, too, with the hymnody of the church. They have been time-tested and tried, not just in rejoicing, but in the most trying times of history. They have stood the test of war, bloodshed, plague, famine, depression, political and economic unrest and upheaval, along with every sin and evil the devil has thrown at Christ's church, yet the gates of Hell have not prevailed. In this liturgy and hymnody stand the sure foundation of the church to withstand these assaults, to look into the pit of sin, death, despair, and darkness and sing with boldness and confidence "Awake, my heart, with gladness, See what today is done; Now after gloom and sadness, Comes forth the glorious sun" (LSB 467).

In them, Christ is delivered and celebrated. He is the church's foundation. He is Her focus and Her hope. Which is exactly why the liturgy and hymnody of the church, handed down through time and generations, not only delivers great Gifts but also protects us. It protects us from passing fads that come and go. It protects us from novelty and "newness" that takes our eyes, our hearts, and our lips away from confessing Christ and His saving Lutheran doctrine. It protects us from ourselves, our sinful nature that wants to make worship, church, and all things about "me." It keeps us "surrounded by so great a cloud of witnesses," like bumpers on a bowling lane, that we would "lay aside every weight, and sin which clings so closely, and let us run with endurance the race that is set before us, looking to Jesus, the founder and perfecter of our faith, who for the joy that was set before him endured the cross, despising the shame, and is seated at the right hand of the throne of God" (Hebrews 12:1-2).

By this doctrine and practice together, we are able to not only "be Lutheran," but "Dare to be Lutheran." These great Gifts of the Word, delivered by the work and practices of the church, can be celebrated and rejoiced boldly and daringly. Seeing the uniqueness and the incredibly sweet comfort of Christ and His Gospel, we do not have to hide our "Lutheranism," but we are able to celebrate it. We put our Lutheran identity, founded in Christ, in the Word, in the Law and Gospel, in the Word and Sacraments, in the practices of the church, up front, first and foremost, unashamed of the Gospel for it is the power of God for your salvation and for the salvation of all (Romans 1:16).

We do not have to apologize for who we are or how we practice our faith. We do not have to be someone or something we are not. We do not need to define ourselves as Roman Catholics or Evangelicals or "not them," but we are Lutheran. We are proud to be Lutheran. We apologize for it only in the sense of a defense and doubling down of the faith. We not only dare to be distinctly Lutheran, but dare to believe and trust that being Lutheran is the very thing that is going to keep and sustain the church, you, and those who follow you in the one, true, saving faith of Jesus Christ.

So be bold, brothers and sisters in Christ. Trust in God's Word and lean not on your own understanding (Proverbs 3:5). Do not be afraid to embrace and put everything you have into God's promises. Dare to believe that being distinctly Lutheran is exactly what you and all the faithful need and is what God wants and how He works to save. Dear brothers and sisters in Christ, "DTBL," dare to be Lutheran.

The Feast for the Unworthy Sinner

Rev. Eli Lietzau

Since the beginning, it has always been about feasting: Perfect Garden with perfect people made in the perfect image of a perfect God, created to feast upon His riches and infinite blessings that were undeserved, yet always freely abundant. Every tree in Eden was planted there specifically for the man and his wife, before they were even spoken into creation by the infinite Word and molded from dust and rib by the unseen hands of the Almighty. "Take and eat of it all, except this one tree right here, for this one isn't for you, it is only for Me," that is what God said to, promised to, the pinnacle of His creation. It was all theirs to delight in and partake of; to feast upon and enjoy; to receive life and rest and everlasting peace… All of it a Gift, forever given and never earned.

And yet Adam and his bride were deceived, for what was good did not seem to be good enough. Instead of delighting in the fruit of the Tree of Life, they desired the fruit of death. Death was never something that they, that we, should have ever known. That knowledge was something that God had kept for Himself, because in order for the finite to know of evil, we must be of it, be one with it, must gorge ourselves until we are bloated to the point of bursting with it. And so to be of evil, to be diseased from conception through the corruption of our flesh, meant that death must come to us, both temporal and eternal. That is the wages of our sin against God: We are now unworthy to partake of His infinite goodness. The Feast must end.

So the Law demands that the Feast be taken from us. The Law declares that the Feast is only for the righteous, only for the perfect, only for the holy, only for those who are good. And goodness, we lost what was good a long, long time ago. And yet this good and gracious God of ours would not have it this way. He would not have His Feast be taken from us. He would not have our unworthiness be the reason why we couldn't partake of the things that He meant for life. He didn't want for us to have to devour the things of death for eternity. The Feast was still to be ours, even if He must be the one who makes it so... But, of course, this should come as no surprise, for He has always been the one to make everything so.

Protoevangelium, the first Gospel, was spoken in the face of that first sinful meal, which corrupted everything that came after it, for there was no time to waste lest the dregs of that cup of death be allowed to forever steal away the Gift of eternal life. But even in that first Gospel promise, we have a glimpse that the Feast was still going to continue forever. "I will put enmity between you and the woman, and between your offspring and her offspring; he shall bruise your head, and you shall bruise his heel" (Genesis 3:15). Where the "bruising" foreshadowed the cross of Calvary and the ancient Serpent's crushed cranium, the word "offspring" germinated the promise of the continued Feast. Both the Hebrew and Septuagint use a word that should more directly be translated as "Seed." And in the context of the Garden of Eden, where trees produced fruit yielding seed, which produced more trees yielding fruit, which were given for mankind to feast upon, we would be remiss to fail to hear the promise that from the Seed of the woman would come the Feast that the fallen sinner would be given to dine upon unto eternal life.

Is it any wonder that the God of Creation, who planted the Garden of which those made in His image could feast, would then plant another Seed to continue the Feast so that those who had lost

His image could have it once again? And so it was that the promise of the Seed produced a Feast of which all of those unworthy sinners who came before it and all of those worthless wretches who would come after could partake.

The promise of God is sure and certain the very moment He speaks it, even if the fulfillment of that promise hasn't yet taken place in the annals of time, for God's Word creates what it says. And so the Old Testament would see the Passover. A lamb slaughtered, its blood painting the threshold of the houses of the terrified sinners who huddled inside. Angel of death passing over those blood-sealed homes while all those within were feasting upon the sacrifice that would keep death at bay. There, we see the Promise of the Garden coming forth in time and space to grant life to sinners whom God called His children. The sacrifice and feast of an innocent lamb foreshadowing the greater sacrifice and Feast of the Innocent Lamb yet still to come.

In that way, the Promise of Eden was given to the people of old: Passover celebrated year after year; Moses and the elders feasted on the mountain of God with God Himself; sacrifices took place daily in the tabernacle and Temple, with the choicest portions consumed by priests and Levites, or even by the people themselves; Prophets like Isaiah and Psalmists like David penned rhyme and verse that spoke of tables prepared in the presence of our enemies and a heavenly feast of rich food and well-aged wine. All of this gifted and granted by the God whose Law demanded the sinner be consumed by the wages of their sin, now freely given to the unworthy sinner so that we might never taste the eternal death that we deserved.

And then, in the fullness of time, God's promised Seed finally came in the flesh, like you and me. As a Lamb, He came uncomplaining forth, conceived in the womb of a fallen sinner by the power of the Holy Spirit. He came so that He might make Himself one with the sinner, full weight of the sinner's sins splashed upon Him in the Jordan River. The Baptizer would point to this Lamb and declare Him to be the one who takes away the sins of the world. The sick would be brought to Him in order to be healed. The lame would be carried to Him that they might run. Those who thirst would come to Him and drink, having rivers of living water flow out of their heart. The multitudes would be fed with miraculous fish and heavenly bread until their bellies were satisfied. The dead would be raised from bed and bier and tomb by the command of His voice.

All of this led to the night in which He was betrayed, as the Lamb of promise would gather His disciples around Him on what would come to be the final Passover. Bread was eaten and wine was drunk, but in this meal a new testament was established. The Passover Feast had found its fulfillment in the Lamb who was to be sacrificed. Both old and new, a lamb was eaten, but on this night that Lamb was God in the flesh. "Take. Eat. This is my body which is given for you. Drink of it, all of you, this cup is the new testament in my blood, which is shed for you for the forgiveness of sin."

It is this Feast that continues on, even to this day. It is the Feast of our Lord, quite literally, the flesh and blood of Christ, given to the starving sinner in time and place. This is how it has always been. In fact, this is the only way that it can ever be. For what could the unworthy ever offer God? What worthiness might we have in ourselves to ever deserve the gracious Gifts that He gives? The One who prepares the Feast doesn't surround His table with those who are worthy. He surrounds Himself precisely with those who are not, with those who are hungry because they can't feed themselves; with those who are thirsty because, try as they might, they can never do enough to quench their sin-parched thirst.

Worthless beggars is all that we are, is all that we could ever be. Empty sacks are the only thing that we bring to the table. But our Lord wouldn't have it any other way, for it is the sick who are in need of a physician, and who among us aren't laden with that sinful disease that leads us to death? Grumbling bellies, that have for far too long gorged themselves on the fruit of that deadly tree, are the only thing that we can offer to God. But such an offering is acceptable to Him, for it comes from a broken heart and a contrite spirit starving for the feast of forgiveness.

Are you hungry? Of course you are! Brought forth in iniquity, your sins are ever before you. They gnaw at your conscience and waste away your inner being. But the promise for you is the same promise that has always been set before the fatally famished fallen. "Take and eat the Feast of your Lord!" It is for you! It is for the starving sinner. It is for the blasphemer and the idolator, for the adulterer and the harlot, the gossip and the liar. The Feast of your Lord is for all those who have been filling their bellies with the things of death. For Christ has already quaffed down to the dregs the cup of God's wrath. He has dined upon your sins and transgressions. He has swallowed up death itself in the eternal victory of the empty tomb. And He desires to lay before you His Feast of righteousness, which makes you one with Him, because He has already taken from you the wretched feast that you have been eating, which threatened to separate you from Him eternally.

And such a Feast, while full and complete, is but a foretaste of the eternal Feast to come. This Feast will sustain you and strengthen you as you walk through the Valley of the Shadow of Death. Fear no evil, for your Shepherd is with you, leading you beside still waters and guiding you to green pastures. Goodness and mercy will follow you all the days of your life. That is His promise to you! And there will be a day when you will dwell in the house of the Lord forever.

I know that sometimes it doesn't feel like it. I know that sometimes the weight of your sins eats at you incessantly. I know that the Specter of death threatens to consume you whole. But the Tree of Life, which is the cross of Christ, has already devoured all of your enemies. Their bite is but transient. Their sting is only temporary. The Feast that is promised to you is an eternal one that you are made worthy to partake of even today for the sake of Christ and Him alone. Right here, in time and space, the Feast of the cross is granted and gifted and eternally given! Delight in this Gift! Receive it often, for it is indeed FOR YOU, both now and for aways!

My fellow starving sinners, my prayer for you is that we will one day sit together at the Wedding Feast of the Lamb in His Kingdom that has no end. That we will dine forever and for always in the new creation of the Garden of Eden. That we will delight eternally in the wonderful Gifts of our Lord… But until that day, let us kneel before our Lord at His table and feast upon Him now, receiving the pledge and token that the eternal "then" is but a heartbeat away! In the name of Jesus!

Rev. William Cwirla

I receive a lot of "junk mail" offering a variety of offers I can't refuse, sales I won't want to miss, and services I can't live without. Some of them probably are good, legitimate deals, and if I chose, I could take advantage of them even though they aren't specifically addressed to me personally. The envelope says, "To the resident of..." and since I'm the resident, it logically must also be addressed to me.

I rarely, if ever, respond to mass mailings. The chief reason is that the sender clearly doesn't know me from Adam. As good as the deal might be, it doesn't grab my attention or interest. I'm nothing more than "resident." They don't even know my name. I could have moved or died, and they would still send their mail to the next. Now, if it were addressed to me personally in the form of a handwritten note, I might be much more inclined to take a look, thinking this deal really might be for me.

Jesus Christ, the Incarnate Son of God, died on the Cross on one good dark Friday, once for all, a single Death that atones for the sin of the world and every sinner in the world. He is the "Lamb of God who takes away the sin of the world" (John 1:29). "He is the atoning sacrifice not only for our sins but for the sins of the whole world" (1 John 2:1-2). Every sin is atoned for in the shed blood of Jesus; every sinner is spoken for in His death.

God could have been content with a general mass-mailed gospel. "To the residents of the world...Jesus Christ died for you." "God so loved the world that He sent His only-begotten Son that whoever believes in Him would not perish but have eternal life" (John 3:16). But does that include me? I'm in the world, and God loved the world; therefore, God must love me. That would be both logical and reasonable.

The trouble is that logic and reason tend to fail us when we are most in despair. When the devil, the unbelieving world, and our own sinful flesh conspire against us, when Sin and Death seem to be closing in all around us, when guilt and shame weigh heavily on our souls, clear thinking and sound reason tend to evaporate like a puddle in the summer heat. Remember what the Small Catechism teaches: "I cannot by my own reason or strength believe in Jesus Christ, my Lord, or come to Him."

"Faith comes by hearing" (Romans 10:17). God doesn't simply broadcast a generic gospel message to the world; He intentionally puts the Gospel into every pair of ears, making them faith-filled ears. God doesn't only announce to the world the forgiveness of sins in Christ, He proclaims it to you, and you need to take that sermon personally. God has you in mind.

For the disciples who first followed Jesus, it began with a personal face-to-face encounter with Jesus, who said to them, "Follow me." Those words from the mouth of the Son of God in the flesh caused the fishermen to leave their boats, nets, and fishing business to follow Jesus as His disciples, and later as His apostles, the first pastors of His church, whose mandate was to make disciples through the preached Word and Baptism (Matthew 28:19-20).

For many of us, our life in Christ began with our Baptism when we were brought to Christ as helpless infants, unable to speak, pray, or decide to follow Jesus. In the water of Baptism, God laid His claim on each of us by name, united us with Christ in His death and life, buried us with Jesus in His tomb, raised us with Jesus in His resurrection, and glorified us in Jesus at the right hand of the Father. The Spirit descended to open our ears, minds, and hearts to receive the

Gifts of Christ in faith. In Baptism, God says "for you" in the water with the Word.

For some of us, it began when a Christian friend, neighbor, or co-worker said to us, "Jesus Christ died for you and for your sins, and for His sake, God is at peace with you and you are forgiven." We heard it as God Himself speaking to us. Perhaps we had known a thing or two about Jesus. We tried reading the Bible a couple of times. Maybe we saw a TV ad that says, "Jesus gets us." In hearing the Gospel in personal "for you" terms, we began to realize that God in Christ is really "for me." He not only "gets me," He forgives me, He loves me. He declares me righteous before God's judgment. He makes me holy and keeps me safely in Christ until I rise from the dead on the Last Day.

The words "for you" take the Gospel as a message and make it a faith-creating reality in our ears, minds, and hearts. The Small Catechism says, "The words 'for you' require all hearts to believe." These words have the power to create the faith they require, and when they have their faith-creating way with us, they prompt us to say a faithful "Amen! This is for me!"

The Large Catechism under the third article of the Creed says this about the "for you" of the Gospel:

> Neither you nor I could ever know anything about Christ, or believe in him and receive him as Lord, unless these were offered to us and bestowed on our hearts through the preaching of the gospel by the Holy Spirit. The work is finished and completed; Christ has acquired and won the treasure for us by his sufferings, death, and resurrection, etc. But if the work remained hidden so that no one knew of it, it would have been all in vain, all lost. In order that this treasure might not remain buried but be put to use and enjoyed, God has caused the Word to be published and proclaimed, in which he has given the Holy Spirit to offer and apply to us this treasure, this redemption. Therefore being made holy is nothing else than bringing us to the Lord Christ to receive this blessing to which we could not have come by ourselves (LC II.38-39, Kolb-Wengert, 436).

Everything that Jesus did to win salvation for the world – His incarnation, life, suffering, death, resurrection, and ascension is offered, delivered, and applied with the words "for you."

Holy Absolution is the "for you" of the Gospel spoken directly into our ears. This is especially true in private Confession and Absolution, where the Pastor forgives the individual by name, and there is no one else hearing it. Even in the general, corporate confession when we confess our sins all together, the Pastor is saying to each of us, "I forgive you all of your sins." That "you" should be heard in the singular. He is talking to you, or more precisely, the Lord is talking to you through him, and you are to hear that voice as Christ Himself speaking to you.

In the Lord's Supper, when we come to the altar to receive the Body and Blood of Christ, the Pastor distributes these Gifts of Christ's sacrifice with the words "Given and shed for you," spoken to each and every communicant. While we commune all together, each of us receives on his or her own tongue the Body and Blood of our Savior from the hand of one called and ordained to represent in His office. It doesn't get more "Christ for you" than that.

The Christian life is a constant remembrance of God's "for you" in Jesus. Every time we open the Scriptures, every time we hear the Absolution, whenever we hear the Word and receive the Body and Blood of Christ, God is speaking His "for you," enlivening and strengthening our faith in Christ, reminding us that God is for us lest we forget.

We are prone to forget. When we absent ourselves from the church, when we no longer hear God's Word or come to the Sacrament and try to go it alone, the devil, the world, and our own flesh quickly rush in to convince us that God is not for us but against us. The world will drive us to despair and to doubt that God even exists, much less cares for us. It will point to all the evil and suffering in the world and ask, "How can God be for you when He allows all of this to happen?" The devil will tempt you to sin in new and ever more destructive ways and then accuse you and say, "How can God be for you when you are such a poor, wretched sinner?" Your old sinful nature, what we call "old Adam," will tempt you to shameful thoughts, desires, words, and deeds, and then your conscience will give you no rest, accusing or making excuses, and telling you, "You're not worthy to be a child of God! You are nothing more than a sinful child of Adam!"

Many people fall away from the church, or avoid it altogether, because they are so filled with guilt or shame that they cannot bear to hear any talk of sin, much less forgiveness. They shut their ears to God's Word, like putting in a pair of noise-canceling earbuds, so they don't hear God speaking His "for you" to them. Instead of faith and love, they become filled with pride, arrogance, hatred, jealousy, anger, and lust. Some try to be "spiritual without being religious" but discover that there is no "God for you" in your own self-cooked spirituality. Some seek new identities in order to become authentically their "true selves," but every self-chosen identity turns out to be another counterfeit, a mask behind which to hide. Some just want to die.

If that description fits you in any way, then you are not alone. That's the "old Adam" in all of us, the original sinner. Welcome to the club! The wonderful news is that Jesus Christ came into this world to save genuine flesh and blood sinners.

"The Word became Flesh and dwelt among us" (John 1:14). The Word is not a concept or an idea, but a Person, the Second Person of the Holy Trinity who took on our flesh, bone, and blood to live our life perfectly from the womb to the tomb, to die our deserved death under the Law, to raise us from the grave, and glorify us in His own flesh at the right hand of God. He came to swap our sin for His righteousness. He became sin for us (2 Corinthians 5:21). Seek Christ in His Word and in His gathered church and know with all certainty that He is there "for you." God has ordained for you to read this article. Take it personally.

If you are a baptized believer in Christ, if you have tasted and seen that the Lord is good, if you regularly hear His Word and are a frequent guest at His Supper, rejoice in the Gifts God has given you and treasure them highly. You are truly blessed! Don't take God's "for you" Gifts lightly. Your forgiveness, life, and salvation literally depend on them, and God, out of the richness of His mercy, has seen to it that your mouth and ears are filled with the Word of Christ.

When you leave the Liturgy, blessed in the Name of God, you go as "little Christs' out into the world. The "Christ for you" in Word and Sacrament is now "Christ for you" on our lips to speak to those around us – those who have never heard, those who have heard and forgotten, those who have heard and didn't believe.

You can say to the world what you have heard for yourself: "Jesus Christ died and rose to save you. God is for you. Believe it."

Rev. Jeffrey Ware

In the summer of 2008, Lutheran youth from across the country gathered for the Higher Things "Amen" conferences. From the beauty of the Poconos in Scranton, PA, to the Gateway to the West in St. Louis, MO, and finally the sandy beaches of Southern California at Concordia University Irvine, 1,713 youth and their chaperones from 93 congregations gathered around Christ's Gifts in worship and catechesis and joined their hearty "amen" with the "amen" of the church throughout the ages. Together they meditated on this one little word and its role in the life of the church. Rooted in the Scriptures of the Old and New Testaments, taught and confessed in Luther's Small Catechism, spoken and sung in churches and homes, at baptisms and funerals, weddings and confirmations, in hospital rooms and in jail cells, this seemingly insignificant word has quite a lot to say for us today.

Children often grow up in the church thinking that the word "amen" means "prayer over." Or perhaps, in the case of meal prayers, "let's eat!" As they mature, they may pick up on the "amen" being a corporate or individual affirmation of what has been proclaimed, confessed, or prayed. From Luther's Small Catechism, they learn that "amen, amen" means "yes, yes, it shall be so." Still, the full significance of this word can be missed in the routine and repetition of prayer and worship.

The youth and adults who attended the "Amen" Higher Things conference in 2008 gained a new appreciation for this word and its importance as the church's affirmation of the truthfulness of God's Word, as an expression of her confidence in God's promises, as a joyful response to receiving God's Gifts, and as a hopeful confidence in a glorious future in eternal life.

Amen! – God's Word Is True

"Amen" in the Hebrew is from a root word meaning "certain, firm, or true," and what could be more certain, firm, or true than God's Word? Jesus affirmed the truthfulness of God's Word when, praying on behalf of His disciples, He asked His Father to "sanctify them in the truth; Your Word is truth" (John 17:17). There it is, from the lips of our Savior Himself! This is His prayer for us, that we would say "amen" to God's Word. When we do, it is a Gift from God, an answer to Jesus' prayer for His church. After all, "Faith comes from hearing, and hearing through the word of Christ" (Romans 10:17).

This is true even when God's Word says things we don't want to hear. In Deuteronomy 27, God commanded the Levites to lead God's people in a liturgy that required them to say "amen" to God's Commandments and to the curses that fall upon those who disobey Him. The liturgy concluded with a final, all-encompassing curse: "'Cursed be anyone who does not confirm the words of this law by doing them.' And all the people shall say, 'Amen'" (Deuteronomy 27:26). That must have been a pretty intense liturgy!

Sometimes the "amen" is hard for us to say. It affirms God's Word to be true, even when it convicts us, even when it uncovers the deeply hidden sins we would prefer to ignore, even when it earns the scornful hatred of a world living in rebellion against it. And yet, the Apostle Paul says, "Let God be true through every one were a liar" (Romans 3:4).

"Amen" is the acknowledgement that God is God and we are not. It's an acknowledgement that we are creatures ("I believe that God has made me and all creatures") and that our Creator knows better than we do what is true and right, holy and just. Our "amen" is the voice of our humble submission to God's Word, and, in our sinful condition, an admission of our failure to be who God created us to be.

The Old Adam rebels against this. He wants to be his own god, the captain of his own destiny, the measure of his own truth. He does not want to repent. He wants to be accepted by God on his own merits, even if it means defying God by watering down His Word and lessening His commands or forsaking them altogether. But, by the sanctifying work of the Holy Spirit, we embrace God's Word in humble submission, recognizing that it is the Word of the Father who loves us, of the Son who redeemed us by His blood, of the Holy Spirit who has given us the Gift of faith, which clings firmly to the promises of His Word.

Amen! - God's Promises Are Sure

The "amen," then, is more than a reluctant affirmation of God's Word or a mere intellectual assent to it. It is the voice of faith, for "faith is the **assurance** of things hoped for, the **conviction** of things not seen" (Hebrews 11:1). Faith looks to Jesus, "the founder and perfecter of our faith, who for the joy that was set before him endured the cross, despising the shame, and is seated at the right hand of the throne of God" (Hebrews 12:2).

"Amen" expresses our confidence in God's promises. Knowing that Jesus was willing to endure the cross for us, we can be sure of God's love. Knowing that Jesus is seated at the right hand of the throne of God, we are convinced that He brings our prayers to our Father and intercedes for us. "For all the promises of God find their Yes in him. That is why it is through him that we utter our Amen to God for his glory" (2 Corinthians 1:20).

Our faith in Jesus is not a blind optimism or naïve hope. It is the deep-rooted assurance, grounded in the cross and resurrection, that God is faithful. Even when doubts arise, when fears assail us, when our guilt and shame threaten to overwhelm us, the "amen" becomes a word we speak to ourselves and to one another, reminding us that God's promises do not depend on the strength of our faith, but on the certainty of His Word. With St. Paul we confidently confess: "The Lord will rescue me from every evil deed and bring me safely into his heavenly kingdom. To him be the glory forever and ever. Amen" (2 Timothy 4:18).

Meanwhile, as dear children ask their dear father, we bring all our concerns to our heavenly Father in prayer. And the "amen" spoken at the conclusion of our prayer is so much more than wishful thinking or a polite ending, but rather, a bold declaration that our prayer is grounded in God's command and promise and is therefore heard by Him and will be answered according to His gracious wisdom. As we learn in the catechism, "This means that I should be certain that these petitions are pleasing to our Father in heaven, and are heard by Him, for He Himself has commanded us to pray in this way and has promised to hear us. Amen, amen means 'yes, yes, it shall be so.'"

Amen! – God's Gifts Are Ours

The "amen" endures in the church's liturgy, prayer, and hymnody as an expression of her faithful certainty that God's Word and promises are true and reliable. But it is also a word expressing confident thankfulness as we receive God's Gifts here and now.

Our "amen" is not spoken to a distant God, who only did great things for us way back when, or who hears our prayers from a "somewhere up there." It is spoken to the God who is present among us with His Gifts. Thus, our "amen" is the receiving word. Christ gives us His Gifts, and we respond "amen," "Thank you. Gift received!"

This "amen" of faith was first given to you in your Baptism, where you were washed "in the name of the Father and of the Son, and of the Holy Spirit, AMEN!" In the baptismal rite, the "amen" is spoken, not just by the pastor but by the entire gathered congregation, the church united, together joyfully affirming the Gifts given in Holy Baptism.

From that moment on, the "amen" became your word of faith, your thanksgiving word, following every gracious Gift of God, and especially those Gifts given in the Divine Service. There, you speak the "amen" as Christ forgives your sins in Holy Absolution, and as He proclaims His Good News to you in Scripture and preaching, in song and confession. There He invites you to His table and feeds you with His own true body ("Amen!") and His own true blood ("Amen!") so that you are strengthened in body and soul to life everlasting ("Amen!"). And finally, the benediction, the Lord's own blessing, and your triple "amen, amen, amen" (Divine Service 3 in *LSB*) of thanksgiving and praise to Father, Son, and Holy Spirit.

Yes, yes, it shall be so. The Word of God is true. The promises of God are certain. Christ's Gifts are for you! And together as His church, we respond with a joyful "amen." Gift received. Thank you! Amen!

Amen! – God's Church Shall Endure

The "amen" endures in our liturgy as our receiving word here and now, and it will endure for all eternity. Perhaps that's why the church never translated the word from the Hebrew. We say our "amen" in continuity with God's people of old, with the church today of every nation, tribe, and tongue, and with the whole heavenly host. We say our "amen" now, knowing that our "amen" will never end.

We have other words that abide in the vocabulary of the church's worship life unchanged and untranslated. Consider the Hebrew words "alleluia" (meaning "Praise the LORD!") and "hosanna" (meaning "save us now"), or the Greek word "kyrie" (meaning "Lord"). The church's retention of such words is an expression of the church's united hope as we await the second coming of our Lord Jesus Christ.

With the saints of old, we cry out to our Lord, "Kyrie eleison" ("Lord have mercy!"); we're not doing very well down here, beset by the temptations of the evil one, surrounded by sin and death. We cry out "Hosanna" ("Save us now!") and remember how Jesus entered Jerusalem to do just that, to give His life for the life of the world and to rise in victory over sin, death, and the devil. "Alleluia" ("Praise the Lord"), Christ is risen! Death is defeated! Christ is making all things new! "On the Last Day, He will raise me and all the dead and give eternal life to me and all believers in Christ. This is most certainly true." Or to put it another way, "Amen!"

That's how the Book of Revelation, the last book of the Bible, ends: "He who testifies to these things says, 'Surely I am coming soon.' Amen. Come, Lord Jesus! The grace of the Lord Jesus be with all. Amen" (22:20-21). In a way, every "amen" spoken by us today is a rehearsal for the great "amen" that will ring out at the consummation of all things. In faith and hope, we say our "amens" here in anticipation of that great day when we shall see with our eyes and know by experience the complete fulfillment of all God's promises. There in the new heavens and the new earth, our "amen" will resound for all eternity!

"Amen" is the church's word, our corporate and individual affirmation of the truthfulness of God's Word, an expression of our confidence in God's promises, a joyful response to the reception of God's Gifts, and a hopeful confidence in the promise of eternal life.

So, don't take it for granted. Don't wait for the pastor to say it for you. Say it with gusto. "Amen" is your word of faith and hope. "May we with saints be numbered where praises never end, / in glory everlasting. Amen, O Lord, Amen!" (*LSB* 941:4).

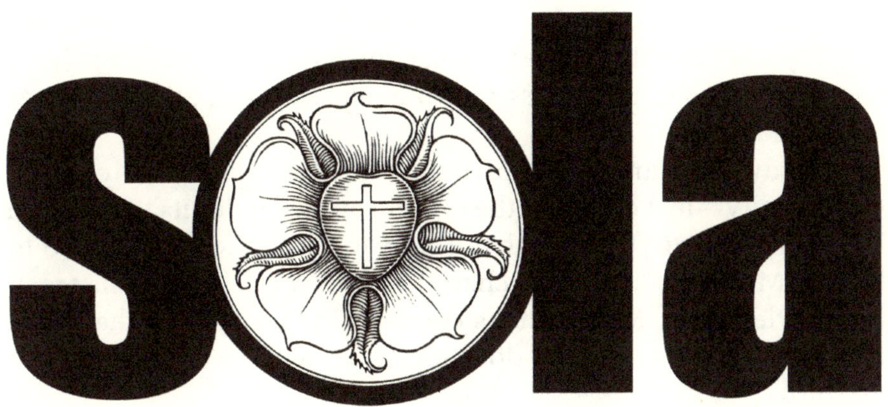

Rev. Bruce Keseman

You gather for the Divine Service with 100 devoted Christians. Are you alone? Of course not. After the service, twenty people remain in the narthex, encouraging you and each other in faith. Are you alone? No. Fifteen minutes later, everyone except you and the custodian has left. Even then, you are not alone. But when that custodian turns out the lights and walks out the door, then you are alone.

Sola means "alone." Not almost alone, but all alone.

Our Lord rescues us from sin's consequences, from death's permanence, from Satan's accusations, and from the Hell we deserve. On account of Christ *alone* by grace *alone* through faith *alone,* taught in Scripture *alone.*

Sola. All alone.

Christ Alone. Solus Christus.

If God graded your life, would you pass? You pass if you have a flawless life. Otherwise, you fail. Alas, everything you and I do has been tainted by our inherited skewedness. *Christ alone* has a flawless life.

Christ alone earns a passing grade. So *Christ alone* does not have to die for His own unholiness.

Yet Jesus dies. He dies because He becomes unholy with our iniquity. He takes the blame for what you have done. Now that Jesus has removed your unholiness, God puts a perfect score on your grade card. And mine.

I saw a chart with thirteen world religions—including Christianity—in a circle. In the middle of the circle sits the Golden Rule ("Whatever you wish that others would do to you, do also to them," Matthew 7:12). The chart assumes that all religions teach the Golden Rule. Maybe that's correct. The problem is that none of us humans consistently does for others what we want them to do for us.

As Romans reminds us, "All have sinned and fall short of the glory of God" (Romans 3:23). Picture you and me running across the roof of a ten-story building because the building caught fire. To escape, we need to jump to the roof of the next building. But 25 feet stand between our roof and that roof. I jump 12 feet across the gap and fall ten stories. You jump 24-1/2 feet of the 25 feet. You barely fall short. But you end up just as dead as I. Similarly, even if some of us make it closer to the glory of God, all of us fall short. We all end up not just dead but damned.

In short, the Golden Rule cannot help us because the Golden Rule cannot get us out of Hell. We need Christ.

If one of the non-Christian religions on the chart I saw provides a savior who lived a perfect life and then used that life to pay your way out of Hell, if one of those religions provides a savior who cracked open his grave with the promise that he will break you out of your grave, then maybe you can put your trust in that person. But no other religion can provide that savior. *Christ alone* has removed your sin. *Christ alone* has undone your death.

That's why Jesus insists, "No one comes to the Father except through Me" (John 14:6). Jesus flies sola. Solus Christus—Christ alone—saves.

Grace Alone. Sola Gratia.

Therefore, salvation must come by *grace alone.*

When I say the name "Gomer," who do you think of? Maybe Gomer Pyle on the old Andy Griffith Show? If you've read the Book of Hosea, you might think of Hosea's wife. Her name is Gomer. But guys, she is not the sort of young woman your parents want you to marry. Gomer works as a prostitute. (By the way, please pity me. At Sola 2009, I had to find a PowerPoint graphic to represent Gomer. I needed to portray her trade and still make the picture appropriate for young children in the audience.)

God told Hosea to marry this sordid woman. Worse, God told Hosea to *purchase* Gomer. Whatever the price, Gomer was not worth the cost. Gomer became Hosea's wife by *grace.* Grace is God's favor when you deserve only God's wrath.

Our Roman Catholic friends teach that grace is a substance that God places in us, so we can do the works that earn God's favor. But according to the Bible, grace does not reside in us. Grace resides in our heavenly Father. Grace is His unmerited attitude toward you and me.

Why does it have to be grace *alone*? Because anything that you or I add will turn God's favor into God's wrath. If I recall correctly, the outdoor temperature at the HT Sola Conference in San Antonio topped 100 degrees. If someone offered me a cool, refreshing drink, I would have accepted gratefully. Unless that someone told me that he spilled a few drops of rat poison in the drink. Even a few drops of poison make the drink unacceptable. Our efforts—because they remain corrupted by our waywardness—add poison to what Christ has done and make us unacceptable to God. So it has to be grace *alone.*

So it's true that "all have sinned and fall short of the glory of God." Now, read the rest of the verse. "And are justified by His grace as a gift, through the redemption that is in Christ Jesus" (Romans 3:23-24). Think about the underlined words. Redemption means you have been bought when you didn't deserve to be bought. Like Gomer. Bought at the cost of Christ's life. It's a *gift. Pure gift. Pure undeserved gift.* Because we are not worth the cost of Jesus' life. Which is why Paul tells us that justification comes by grace.

To understand justification, think of a courtroom. God sits as the Judge. You are the defendant. You know you're guilty. The Judge knows you're guilty. But your defense attorney says, "Charge my client's crimes to my account." The Judge answers, "Then you'll have to serve the sentence. You'll be damned to Hell." Your attorney replies, "For the joy set before Me, it would be my privilege to serve that sentence. In fact, Your Honor—Father—I already served the sentence." So the Father drops His gavel and declares, "I find the defendant not guilty by reason of Jesus."

That's justification. By grace. *Grace alone.*

Faith Alone. Sola Fide.

You could tell me, "All you have to do is believe and you'll receive the benefits of God's grace." But that's like telling a dead woman in a casket, "All you have to do is sit up and you'll be alive." The statement may be true, but doing it is impossible. Dead people cannot do anything except stay dead. Not one of us can believe in Jesus Christ our Lord or come to Him, because we enter this world spiritually dead. Ephesians says so: "You were *dead* in the trespasses and sins in which you used to live" (Ephesians 2:1-2, my emphasis).

Two EMTs roll a dead woman into the emergency room. This ER has life-restoration serum. (I just invented life-restoration serum for this story.) The woman only needs to connect an IV tube from the life-restoration serum to her body. But the woman cannot hook up the IV tube because she is dead. However, a nurse can connect an IV line.

God provides various IV bags: Scripture proclamation, Baptism, Absolution, and Communion. He fills each with life-restoration serum from Christ's perfect life, sacrificial death, and victorious resurrection. Faith is the IV tube that receives what *Christ alone* did. But we cannot connect the IV tube. We cannot create faith in ourselves because we are dead in our trespasses. But the Holy Spirit can hook up the IV tube. The Holy Spirit can give me faith. The Holy Spirit can call you by the Gospel and enlighten you with His Gifts. And He does.

That means Roman Catholicism errs when it teaches that we must add our works to faith in order to be saved. That would not be faith *alone*. Plus, remember that any works we try to add, because they remain tainted by sin, will hinder our salvation, not lead to our salvation. Likewise, some Protestants err when they claim God provides grace and then we provide faith. We can't provide faith because we are spiritually stillborn.

Notice that faith does not do anything to be saved. Like an IV tube, saving faith simply receives what is given to it. Saving faith is totally passive. (If you forgot the difference between active and passive, ask your English teacher or Google it.) But once Jesus' life begins flowing in us, once faith receives the benefits of Christ's occupied cross and empty tomb, then faith becomes active. Then faith not only *receives* the forgiveness and life of Jesus, but faith also begins to love God and to care for people. Our good works do not lead to our salvation. Our good works result from the salvation that has been given to us. They flow from *faith alone,* faith through which Christ's life restoration serum flows to you.

Scripture Alone. Sola Scriptura.

"Everything that I command you, you shall be careful to do. You shall not add to it or take from it" (Deuteronomy 12:32). Why does God warn not to add to or take away from His Word? Because when we add to it or subtract from it, it ceases to be God's Word. Then it ceases to be sure and certain. We need *Scripture alone.* That's *sola Scriptura.*

What is the source of what your church teaches and you believe? Roman Catholicism takes its teachings from Scripture but also from apostolic teaching that has been passed down through the church. That's not *Scripture alone.* But don't Lutherans take our teachings from Scripture and the writings of Martin Luther? No! That would be adding to God's Word. We take our teachings from *Scripture alone.* We accept the writings of Martin Luther (and other teachers of the church) only if they teach what Scripture teaches.

Remember what happened when Paul and his fellow missionaries preached in Berea? The people "received the word with all eagerness, examining Scriptures daily to see if these things were so" (Acts 17:11). They did not say, "I believe the message because it came from an apostle or from a pastor I trust." They did not say, "I believe it because it comes from tradition or from Martin Luther." Paul preached as an apostle, but the Bereans still made sure his message matched the Bible. Make sure the message that your pastor teaches and the message that this essay teaches completely match what the Bible teaches. We need *Scripture alone*. Nothing added.

And nothing subtracted. In the 1970s, the Lutheran Church-Missouri Synod split because teachers claimed you cannot believe everything the Bible teaches. They used reason to determine whether or not to believe a passage. For example, it seems far-fetched to believe that Jonah was swallowed and then puked out by a big fish. Please do not believe only what seems logical. It does not seem logical—yet it is true and essential to our salvation—that Jesus was born of a virgin, that Jesus paid our debt by being murdered, and that Jesus broke open our graves by walking out of His tomb alive three days after they laid him in that tomb dead.

Maybe you know that Thomas Jefferson removed from his Bible anything that he deemed miraculous. Maybe you know that so-called scholars in the Jesus Seminar (perhaps it should be called the Anti-Jesus Seminar) met to decide what words in the Gospels Jesus actually spoke (As if they were there to hear Jesus speak). They voted that Jesus did not teach the Lord's Prayer, although most agreed that He probably prayed the word "Father."

Pay attention to 2 Timothy: "All Scripture is *breathed* out by God" (2 Timothy 3:16). Remember how God *breathed* life into Adam? God also breathes life—Christ's life—into the Scriptures. The Bible contains exactly the life-giving words that God wants you to know.

When you go to the library, you'll find fact books and fiction books. The Bible is a fact book. So is your math book. But the Bible is more than a fact book. The Bible is a faith book. It is written so you can believe: "These are written that you may *believe* that Jesus is the Christ, the Son of God, and that by *believing* you may have <u>life</u> in His name" (John 20:31).

That's because the Scriptures testify about Jesus (see John 5:39). The Bible takes the witness stand and tells the truth about what *Christ alone* has done for you. Add to the Bible or take from the Bible, and you no longer have God's reliable words of truth. But when you have *Scripture alone*, you can believe everything the Bible says. Without doubt.

Most people say we are born with life. In reality, we are born with death waiting to happen. We've all been dying since the day our parents conceived us. Our Lord reverses that death and replaces it with His life. On account of Christ alone. Because only Jesus has done what is necessary to save us. By grace alone through faith alone. Because anything we try to add would turn God's favor into God's wrath. By Scripture alone. Because when nothing has been added or subtracted, you can believe the Bible implicitly.

Christ alone. Grace alone. Faith alone. Scripture alone. Not *almost* alone. Completely alone. Sola.

GIVEN

Dr. John Pless

The Apostle Paul says, “What do you have that you have not received?” (1 Corinthians 4:7). The Christian life does not begin with what we do but with what we have been given. We do not start with our obligations but with what God has given us.

God has given us Himself; therefore, we are not to make for ourselves any counterfeit gods. Just prior to giving the children of Israel the Ten Commandments, God announced, “I am the Lord your God.” With these words, God declares Himself to be our God and Lord. We do not choose Him to be our God; He has chosen us to be His people.

The First Commandment and the First Article of the Creed overlap. The one true God is our Creator and more. The Large Catechism reminds us that to confess God as Creator is “the shortest possible way of describing and illustrating the nature, will, acts, and work of God the Father” (LC II:10, K-W, 432). The God who gives Himself to us to be feared, loved, and trusted above all things is the God who made all that exists.

For Luther, the confession that God is the Maker of heaven and earth is not an abstraction. It is not a generic assertion that God is an "unmoved mover," the architect of the universe, or the primal cause. A Lutheran theologian of the last century, Helmut Thielicke, wisely raised the question: "Do we understand, then, why it is such a liberation to hear Luther begin his explanation, *not* with light years and dizzying thought of space, but rather with the simple statement, 'I believe that God has created *me*?"[1] The Christian confession of creation is cosmic in scope, embracing all that God has made, but it is also intensely personal: God has made me. My life, so little when compared to the vastness of the universe, was uniquely made by the same God who created stars and planets beyond our feeble imagination.

The First Article is the recognition that this God has made me and all creatures. God gives, we receive. The Small Catechism spells this out in detail:

> "God has made me and all creatures…He has **given** my body and soul, eyes, ears, and all my members, my reason and all my senses… He also **gives** me the things I need to support this creaturely life like food, clothing, family, and a place to live. He defends, guards, and protects all out of His fatherly, divine goodness and mercy without any merit or worthiness on my part."

It is all gift! God is the Giver, and we are those who are given to. Again from the Large Catechism:

> "For this reason we ought daily to practice this article, impress it upon our minds, and remember it in everything we see and in every blessing that comes our way. Whenever we escape distress or danger, we should recognize how God gives and does all of this so that we may sense and see in them his fatherly heart and his boundless love toward us. Thus our hearts will be warmed and kindled with gratitude to God and a desire to use all these blessings to his glory and praise"(LC II:23, K-W, 433).

---

[1] Helmut Thielicke, *Man in God's World* edited and translated by John W. Doberstein (New York : Harper & Row, 1965), 24.

God was not under an obligation to create us. Creation is an act of His everlasting love in Christ.

We do not rightly know the Creator apart from Christ Jesus. It is in Christ that we see the fatherly heart of Christ. It is only through Christ's suffering, death, and resurrection that we receive the good things of this creation. The Second Article of the Creed portrays the Father's eternal Son, who was born of the Virgin Mary, to be my Lord. For Luther, Lord is a gift word.[2]

The Father gave His Son into our world of dust and death to save us from condemnation (see John 3:16). He came in our flesh to be our Lord. Luther sees the very core of the Creed, this simple confession: "I believe that Jesus Christ, true Son of God, has become my Lord" (LC II:27, K-W, 434). How has Jesus become my Lord? We do not make Jesus our Lord by our choice of Him over other lords or by our obedience. He has made Himself my Lord by His work for me, redeeming me, a lost and condemned person, purchasing me with His blood and winning a battle against sin, death, and the devil that I could only lose. Luther unpacks this in the Large Catechism: "It means that he has redeemed and released me from sin, from the devil, from death, and from all misfortune. Before this I had no lord or king but was captive under the power of the devil. I was condemned to death and entangled in sin and blindness" (LC II:27, K-W, 434).

To have Jesus as Lord is to be on the receiving end of His grace and favor. It is to live under Him in His kingdom and serve Him in everlasting righteousness, innocence, and blessedness here in time and hereafter in eternity, for He forever lives and reigns as our Brother and Savior. This is the Gift of redemption, reconciliation with God. It was accomplished for the whole world in the cross and resurrection of Christ Jesus.

---

[2] Robert Kolb notes that Luther uses a variety of images such as Meditator, Helper, Comforter, Mercy Seat, Bishop, Shepherd, Brother, Intercessor, Gift, and Deliverer in addition to Vicar (vicarious sacrifice) and Victor to express what Christ means "for us." See Robert Kolb, "Martin Luther on the Atonement" in *Luther's Large Catechism with Annotations and Contemporary Applications*, ed. John T. Pless and Larry M. Vogel (St. Louis: Concordia Publishing House, 2022), 380.

Redemption was done, but it must be delivered. Christ acquired the gift, but it must be given. This is the work of the Holy Spirit. He takes what Jesus has done for you and hands it over to you (see John 14:26; 16:13-15). Luther puts it like this:

> "Neither you nor I could ever know anything about Christ, or believe in him and receive him as Lord, unless these were offered to us and bestowed on our hearts through the preaching of the gospel by the Holy Spirit. The work is finished and completed; Christ has acquired and won the treasure for us by his sufferings, death, and resurrection, etc. But if the work remained hidden so that no one knew of it, it would have all been in vain, all lost. In order that this treasure might not remain buried but be put to use and enjoyed, God has caused the Word to be published and proclaimed, in which he has given the Holy Spirit to offer and apply to us this treasure, this redemption. Therefore being made holy is nothing else than bringing us to the Lord Christ to receive this blessing, to which we could not have come by ourselves" (LC II:38-39, K/W, 436).

The Holy Spirit's bestowal of Christ's Gifts is not a one-time affair. He keeps at it time and time again as the Small Catechism delights to affirm: "In this Christian Church He daily and richly forgives my sins and the sins of all believers." The Spirit works through Baptism to give the new birth of water and the Word (see Titus 3:5-8; John 3:5). Far more than an initiation rite into the church, the Gift of Baptism is a Gift that keeps on giving. It is present tense, not just "I was baptized" but "I am baptized." Baptism enfolds the Christian's life in constant repentance and faith, marking a daily dying to sin and a daily rising again to the newness of life in Christ.

The Smalcald Articles reminds us that God is generously giving His Gifts in more than one way: "We now want to return to the gospel, which gives guidance and helps against sin in more than one way, because God is extravagantly rich in his grace" (SA III.4, K-W, 319). God gives forgiveness of sins through the preached Word, Baptism, the Sacrament of the Altar, the Office of the Keys, and the words of forgiveness and consolation on the lips of brothers and sisters in Christ. God has more than one way to give you His precious gifts.

The words that the Lord uses to institute the Sacrament of the Altar (see Matthew 26:28; Mark 14:22-24; Luke 22:19-20; 1 Corinthians 11:23-25) might be described, as Luther did, as "the Gospel in a nutshell," for they proclaim the death of Christ as the new testament where you are named an heir. In his explanation of the Sacrament of the Altar, Luther accents the "FOR YOU." With His Body and Blood under bread and wine, you are given the forgiveness of your sins.

While it is not a Means of Grace, there is another Gift that God has given you. It is prayer. God has given us His name in Baptism so that we may call upon Him anytime and anywhere. In the Scriptures, God does four things with His name. First, He identifies or reveals Himself (see Exodus 3:13-14). Second, God locates Himself (see Exodus 20:24; 1 Kings 8:27-29; Matthew 18:20). Third, God blesses (see Numbers 6:22-27). Fourth, God gives us access to Himself (see Acts 2:21). Because of Jesus' death and resurrection, we have boldness and confidence to call upon His Father as our Father. The prayer which Jesus has given us, the Lord's Prayer, demonstrates the comprehensiveness of God's Gifts for body and soul, enabling us to pray with the certainty that God hears us and answers us according to His good and gracious will (see Ephesians 3:14-21).

We are also given faith. As the Catechism, which is the pattern of sound words drawn from Scripture (see 2 Timothy 1:13), understands it, faith is the recognition that all that we have and all that we are is a Gift from the Father for the sake of His Son. The Christian life is first and foremost not about our giving but our receiving. It is only because we have been given to by the Triune God that we can give Him "thanks and praise" each day and that we can "serve and obey" Him not by retreating from the world but by devoting ourselves to the needs of the neighbor in our various earthly callings (see the Table of Duties in the Small Catechism).

We give because God has first given to us. This truth was nicely illustrated by the Lutheran hymnwriter, Paul Gerhardt, in his will to his one surviving son: "Do good to people, even if they cannot repay you back because...." The reader expects that the sentence will continue with: "God *will* repay you." Paul Gerhardt frustrates this expectation by continuing "...for what human beings cannot repay, the Creator of heaven and earth *has* repaid you long ago when he created you, when he gave you his only Son. And when he accepted and received you in Holy Baptism as his child and heir."[3]

[3] Oswald Bayer, "Justification: Basis and Boundary of Theology" in *By Faith Alone: Essays in Honor of Gerhard O. Forde,*ed. Joseph Burgess and Marc Kolden (Grand Rapids: Eerdmans, 2004), 70-71

Peace be With You!

Rev. Brent Kuhlman

You know how it works in the world and especially in your own life. You sin against someone and that person sins right back at you—in spades. As he clenches his fists, he shouts: "You hurt me! I'll harm you even more! I'll mess you up! Bigly! You are going to get what you deserve!" Tit for tat. *Quid pro quo*. Right? Tragically—of course! The world and the old Adam are very good at it. In fact, the world and our old-Adamic natures have perfected it. No mercy. No forgiveness. Revenge. Payback. Settling scores.

That takes me to John 20:19-23. Lord and God Jesus is freshly and bodily risen from the grave. It is Easter evening. He has been sinned against. And by his own disciples in fact! Peter, for example, denied Jesus three times. When Jesus was arrested, the disciples ran. Now they have locked themselves up in a room (bolted the door), afraid of being hunted down, arrested, and jailed for associating with Him.

Then, all of a sudden, without even knocking or asking for permission, the resurrected Jesus shows up in the midst of these cowering sinners. Can you imagine the panic? The anxiety? "What will he do with us? What will he say to us? He is the one we sinned against! He is the one we hurt! Will he give us what we deserve? What have we earned because of our sin?"

Check it out. Lord and God Jesus preaches one of the most remarkably delicious sermons for sinners that He ever preached in the New Testament: "Peace be with you," (John 20:19; cf. the angels' sermon at Jesus' birth: "Glory to God in the highest, and on earth PEACE among those with whom he is pleased," Luke 2:14. Peace is his cup of tea!). LORD GOD JESUS FORGIVES THEM! He absolves these sinners. He is not at war with them. He is not out for revenge against them. No tit for tat! No *quid pro quo*! From Lord and God Jesus' mouth, they hear: "Peace be with you." His word of peace gives what it says.

The forgiveness that Jesus won and achieved on the cross for all sinners gets delivered and bestowed upon these sinners by Lord and God Jesus himself. That is why he shows them his hands and his side. They are his sacrifice-for-all-sin-Good-Friday-wounds. Isaiah calls them "healing" wounds (Isaiah 53:5; cf. 1 Peter 2:24) – or forgiveness-for-sinner-wounds because from them flowed his blood that cleanses or purifies from all sin (1 John 1:7). These are the wounds from which the divine peace/forgiveness comes!

This fear-filled, locked-in-a-room crew of sinners stands before Lord and God Jesus, and He categorically forgives them through his word of "peace be with you." Dr. Luther astutely and most helpfully states that, "in this greeting is contained the entire Gospel," (LW 69:343)! Indeed. After all, his "peace be with you" means their sins are forgiven. They are redeemed from death. His suffering is for them. His resurrection is theirs. It is no wonder then that "the disciples were glad when they saw the Lord" (John 20:20).

Jesus speaks another "peace be with you" (John 20:21). With the gospel, there is always more. It is overflowing and abundant. Lord and God Jesus breathes on them and gives them the Holy Spirit to equip them for a specific task. And what is that? Well, just as the Father sent Jesus, he now sends them as his authorized apostolic ambassadors to speak his word of forgiveness to other sinners and open heaven's door. "If you forgive the sins of any, they are forgiven them," (John 20:23). Jesus says in a parallel passage found in Matthew 16:19,

"I will give you the keys of the kingdom of heaven, ... and whatever you loose on earth shall be loosed in heaven." See also Matthew 18:18. However, if someone stubbornly and unrepentantly refuses to use the wounds and words of Jesus properly for forgiveness, if they purposely want to answer for their sin by their own blood and not the blood of Jesus, then the authorized apostolic ambassador of Lord and God Jesus will withhold forgiveness: "if you withhold forgiveness from any, it is withheld," (John 20:23). The other way Jesus puts it is in the way of Matthew 16:19; 18:18: "whatever you bind on earth shall be bound in heaven."

Lord and God Jesus' breath. His words. His Spirit. His peace/forgiveness. The sins the sent ones loose or forgive are loosed and forgiven. What they bind or retain is bound and retained. As certain on earth as though Lord and God Jesus himself were speaking. In fact, He is and does. That's the nature of apostolic ministry. "He who hears you, hears me," (Luke 10:16).

In John 20:19-23, we observe that Jesus guarantees that his voice will be heard in the church until he reappears visibly in glory on the Last Day to judge the living and the dead. One of the ways we hear his living voice (*viva vox Christi*) is in Holy Absolution. The church confesses that the Absolution "is not the voice or word of the person speaking it, but it is the Word of God, who forgives sin. For it [the Absolution] is spoken in God's stead and by God's command.... [and] that God requires us to believe this absolution as much as if it were God's voice resounding from heaven," (AC XXV, 72:3-5). So, what we have here in John 20 is not simply the sending of a few, but the establishment of an office, the office of the holy ministry. Pastors are commanded by the Lord in John 20 to forgive the sins of penitent sinners and to withhold forgiveness from the unrepentant as long as they do not repent.

I will never forget what happened in an LCMS congregation a few decades ago. The event is tattooed on my brain. In the future, if I get dementia and am restricted to a care facility, I will still remember and tell you when you come to visit me. Here is how it went down. The pastor went on vacation for three weeks. For the first two Sundays, the substitute clergyman deleted the preparatory part of the Divine Service – Confession and Absolution. Guess what he did on the third Sunday? That's right. You guessed it! The same! It was at that point that an elderly woman in the congregation immediately interrupted: "Pastor! This is the third Sunday in a row that you have not absolved us. Now turn to page such and such in the hymnal and DO IT!" She could not live without Lord and God Jesus' forgiveness in the way that he mandated it in John 20. Faithfully, she clung to the "peace be with you" from Prince of Peace Jesus himself through the pastor.

Can a pastor forgive? I'm asked that all the time. The answer is: YES! However, the forgiver is Jesus. He simply uses the pastor as his mouth to speak his word of peace/forgiveness. That is precisely why the pastor says: "In the stead and by the command of my Lord Jesus Christ I forgive you all your sins in the name of the Father and of the Son and of the Holy Spirit," (*LSB*, 291, 293; cf. 151, 167, 185, 203, 214).

Is there divine authority upon the earth to forgive sins? That's what astounded the people when Jesus forgave the paralyzed man. "My son, your sins are forgiven" (Matthew 9:2; Mark 2:5). Who forgives sin? Lord and God Jesus does! And one of the ways he speaks and delivers his Good Friday forgiveness to sinners until the end of time, is through Holy Absolution, spoken by those whom Jesus himself has authorized and sent with his Word and Spirit.

Again, I remind you of what Jesus promised in a sending before the John 20 account that is recorded in Luke 10:16, "He who hears you, hears me." This is why the church teaches that when pastors "offer the Word of Christ or the sacraments, they offer them in the stead and place of Christ," (Ap, VII-VIII, 178.28)—understood properly in the way the apostle Paul teaches in 2 Corinthians 5:20, saying, "therefore we are ambassadors for Christ, God making his appeal through us." The Small Catechism faithfully teaches that we are to "receive absolution, that is forgiveness, from the pastor as from God Himself, not doubting, but firmly believing that by it [the absolution] our sins are forgiven before God in heaven," (*LSB*, 326).

Forgiveness. That's what it's all about. Forgiveness achieved and won in the very good, Good Friday afternoon death of Lord and God Jesus on the cross. "In Christ God was reconciling the world to himself, not counting their trespasses against them," (2 Corinthians 5:19). Salvation accomplished: "It is finished!" (John 19:30).

Now risen from the dead, Jesus sees to it that the forgiveness he attained and accomplished gets delivered. That is John 20:19-23. Forgiveness from him is to be spoken and delivered in the speaking.

This is the gift of the resurrection of Jesus. What was won on the cross is now packaged for delivery. Forgiveness won for all on Calvary is forgiveness delivered by the speaking of forgiveness – Holy Absolution.

In John 20, Lord and God Jesus binds his words to their words. His breath to their breath. It is his peace. It is his forgiveness to be spoken in his church by his office. This is why the pastor asks: "Do you believe that my forgiveness is God's forgiveness?" ("Individual Confession and Absolution," *LSB*, 293). "Do you believe that the forgiveness I speak is not my forgiveness but God's?" ("Corporate Confession and Absolution, *LSB*, 291). That's the question of Holy Absolution. To which faith says: Yes!

Faith comes by hearing the living voice of Christ (*viva vox Christi* / Romans 10:17). Consequently, Lord and God Jesus has arranged for your hearing him. How do you know for certain you are forgiven? Jesus says so. You hear him when the pastor absolves you: "Upon this your confession, I, by virtue of my office, as a called and ordained servant of the Word, announce the grace of God unto all of you, and in the stead and by the command of my Lord Jesus Christ I forgive you all your sins in the name of the Father and of the Son and of the Holy Spirit," (*LSB*, 185).

What do you believe according to John 20:19-23? You have it memorized. It is tattooed on your brain too just like mine. The Small Catechism's answer and your answer is:

> "I believe that when the called ministers of Christ deal with us by His divine command, in particular, when they exclude openly unrepentant sinners from the Christian congregation and absolve those who repent of their sins and want to do better, this is just as valid and certain, even in heaven, as if Christ our dear Lord dealt with us Himself" (*LSB*, 326).

When you hear Holy Absolution, you are standing before Lord and God Jesus (*coram Deo*), and you hear his voice. As you believe the John 20 "peace be with you" in Holy Absolution, so you have! His words do and give what they say!

The peace of the Lord be with you.

In the Name of Jesus.

The Church's Number

Rev. Kurt Onken

The number 12 is a familiar number. There are 12 months in a year. 12 inches in a foot. 12 hours on our clocks and watches. Doughnuts are often bought by the dozen … 12 delectable deep-fried delights! Here in Washington, no player on our NFL football team – the Seattle Seahawks – is allowed to wear the number 12. That number is reserved for the fans who have come to be known as "The Twelves" and who boisterously support the 11 men on the gridiron.

God seems to like the number 12. It appears in many different places in the Bible. It's the number of the church. We are the Lord's "Twelves" because he is the one who creates the church, calling people to faith in Jesus through the gospel.

God Creates the 12

God first made promises to the Patriarchs, our ancient fathers in faith ... Abraham, Isaac, and Jacob. He promised to bless them and their offspring, to make a great nation from them, and that all families of the earth would be blessed through them (Genesis 12:1-3; 15:5; 26:4; 28:14). Jacob's 12 sons became the 12 tribes of Israel (Genesis 35:22-26).

Jacob's son Joseph gets most of the attention in Genesis. The account begins with his jealous brothers selling him to a group of traders going down to Egypt. The Lord blesses Joseph there, and Joseph eventually becomes right-hand man to Pharaoh, the king of Egypt, and saves the land from the ravages of a famine (Genesis 37-50). However, it was through the descendants of Jacob's son Judah that the promise given to Abraham is kept (Genesis 49:8-12) because Judah's most important descendant is our Savior, Jesus.

Joseph settled his family in Egypt, but after his death, a new king arose and enslaved the Israelites (Exodus 1:8-14). After about 400 years, God intervened and rescued Israel from their bondage. He called Moses to lead the people out from Pharaoh's grasp. He takes the initiative in establishing a relationship with them, as he said when he gave them the Ten Commandments: "I am the LORD your God, who brought you out of the land of Egypt, out of the house of slavery" (Exodus 20:2), and later, "The LORD your God has chosen you to be a people for his treasured possession, out of all the peoples who are on the face of the earth" (Deuteronomy 7:6).

The Sad History of the 12

Sadly, the 12 tribes of Israel were constantly unfaithful to the Lord. They repeatedly rebelled against him. They complained and grumbled during their wilderness wanderings after God so powerfully delivered them from their slavery in Egypt. They made a golden calf and worshiped it. Once they settled in the land of Canaan, they lived just like the other nations around them, worshiping other false gods and even sacrificing their children to the Canaanite god Molech (Jeremiah 32:35). They cried out for a king and, in so doing, rejected God as their king (1 Samuel 8:7).

After Kings Saul, David, and Solomon, the nation was divided. The Northern Kingdom, Israel, was destroyed by the Assyrians, and the people scattered. The Southern Kingdom, Judah, was destroyed by the Babylonians, who took the people into exile for 70 years. The time between the Old and New Testaments was a further time of conflict: rule by the Greeks, brief independence for Judea, and then rule by the Romans at the time of the birth of Jesus.

Despite the rebellion of the Israelites, God determined to preserve a faithful remnant in keeping with his promises (Isaiah 46:3-4). Yet even those among the remnant were still sinners in need of a Savior.

12 Narrowed Down to 1

Jesus came to be the perfect Israelite, 12 narrowed down to 1, the one truly faithful remnant, made like us in every way but without sin (Hebrews 4:15). He came to do what the people of Israel were unable to do, to do what you and I are unable to do … to live a perfectly obedient, faithful life, and to give his life as a ransom for many (Matthew 20:28). Jesus is the descendant of Eve who would crush the Serpent's head (Genesis 3:15) through his death and resurrection. He is the descendant of Abraham through whom "all the families on the earth shall be blessed" (Genesis 12:3). He is the descendant of Judah who would come to rule and reign as the King of Kings (Genesis 49:9-10; Revelation 5:5). He is the Son of David whose rule will last forever (2 Samuel 7:11-16). He is the Suffering Servant of Isaiah 53, the one who was "pierced for our transgressions" and "crushed for our iniquities. Upon him was the chastisement that brought us peace, and with his stripes we are healed" (Isaiah 53:5).

Jesus Recreates the 12

Jesus fulfilled God's promises to the people of Israel and recreated the 12 by calling 12 apostles to spread His message. They are the "sent ones." That's what an apostle is … one sent with a commission, a message, much like the way an ambassador to a foreign country today brings word from the leader of the nation from which he or she comes. The apostles were sent to proclaim repentance and forgiveness of sins to all nations in the name of Jesus Christ (Matthew 28:19-20; Acts 2:38).

The Israelites did not choose God but were chosen by him to be a unique people and nation in order to bring about the Savior. Likewise, throughout the New Testament, the church is described as having been chosen (for example, John 15:16; Ephesians 1:3-4, et. al.) and called (for example, Romans 1:6-7; Romans 8:28-30; 1 Corinthians 1:2; 1:9; 2 Timothy 1:8-10, et. al.). God is the one who always takes the initiative. This is true for believers in Christ the Savior today, that is, members of the holy Christian church by Baptism and faith. We do not choose God, but he chooses us. We proclaim the Savior who has already come and who still comes to us today through his Word and Sacraments, and he sends his church out with the apostolic message of repentance and forgiveness of sins in the name of Jesus.

12: The New Israel

In the New Testament, we also find descriptions of the church which are very similar to the way Old Testament Israel was described. Compare the way God speaks to the Israelites in Exodus with the way Peter describes the church:

"...you shall be to me a kingdom of priests and a holy nation. These are the words that you shall speak to the people of Israel" (Exodus 19:6).

"But you are a chosen race, a royal priesthood, a holy nation, a people for his own possession..." (1 Peter 2:9; compare also Deuteronomy 7:6 quoted above).

Compare the way the prophet Hosea foresees the creation of a new people with Peter's further description of the church in the verse immediately after the one above:

"I will show my love to the one I called 'Not my loved one.' I will say to those called 'Not my people,' 'You are my people'; and they will say, 'You are my God'" (Hosea 2:23 NIV).

"Once you were not a people, but now you are God's people; once you had not received mercy, but now you have received mercy" (1 Peter 2:10).

The Old Testament people of God were saved in the same way that the New Testament people of God are saved ... by faith in God's promises. Romans 4 makes that perfectly clear when it describes the way Abraham was declared righteous in God's sight. It was not by his bloodline. It was not because he had received the covenant of circumcision. It was by faith! And the same is true today. Those who are righteous by faith in Christ are the true descendants of Abraham. Paul calls Abraham "the father of us all" (Romans 4:16).

What about Jewish people today? Paul addresses this in the ninth through eleventh chapters of Romans. They can become members of the 12, the holy Christian church, by faith in Christ, just like you and me. Believing Jews and Gentiles are the True Israel of God (Galatians 6:14-16).

The 12s of Revelation

The last place we discover the number 12 and its multiples is in the last book of the Bible, the Revelation to St. John. The Book of Revelation gives us God's heavenly perspective of the church in its present tribulation, while facing persecution, and also in its future glory.

In Revelation 4:1-4, John sees 24 elders seated on thrones, clothed in white, and wearing golden crowns. These most likely are representatives of God's people of the Old and New Testaments (12 tribes and 12 apostles).

Then, in Revelation 7:4-12, John hears about 144,000 who are the servants of God with a seal on their foreheads, a mark of belonging ... like the sign of the cross we receive in Baptism. One hundred forty-four thousand is 12 times 12 times 1,000. The first 12 represents believers prior to Jesus' birth who trusted in God's promise of a Messiah to come. The second 12 represents believers after Jesus' birth and ministry who trusted in the Messiah who has already come. Multiply the two together, then by 1,000 (a number symbolizing the completion of God's plans and timing), and you have 144,000. This does not mean that there are only going to be 144,000 people in heaven. If that were the case, heaven would have been filled a long time ago! Besides, in the verses following this section, we read how John saw "a great multitude that no one could number." Thankfully, rather than a literal number, 144,000 is symbolic of the total number of all believers in Christ across time ... "a great multitude that no one could number" (Revelation 7:9).

The number 12 appears again in Revelation 21 when the Holy City, the New Jerusalem, descends from heaven as a bride dressed for her wedding day. This is a picture of the Last Day when the risen and ascended Jesus visibly returns and receives his bride, the church, to be with him in eternity. This holy and heavenly city has—count 'em—12 gates and 12 foundations with the names of the Apostles written on them. The city is a gigantic cube measuring 12,000 stadia high, deep, and broad. This is a reminder of how the Holy of Holies in the tabernacle, and later the temple, was also a cube. The Holy of Holies was the place behind the curtain where God's gracious presence rested above the Ark of the Covenant. Here, this cubic heavenly city is likened to the Holy of Holies in its entirety, the place where God's church enjoys God's presence forever. And finally, the city is pictured as having walls 144 cubits high—again, 12 times 12—a place of peace and safety for eternity.

12: The Church's Number

God creates his 12, the church. God calls the church together from among all people across all time and places. God rescues His church from sin, death, and the devil in Christ. God brings His church into relationship with him in Holy Baptism and gives us faith to trust in Jesus. God sends His church to proclaim the message of Christ crucified and risen for the forgiveness of sins. Even though the church endures trouble and persecution in this life, she reigns with Christ Jesus now and will reign with him in eternity.

God loves the number 12.

He loves you!

From Above

Dr. Carl Fickenscher

As the conversation began, Nicodemus only knew what we all know.

> "Things are looking up!" "The market is up." "Surf's up!"
>
> On a good day, we feel up. Some poor souls desperate for a good day want to get high—even if it dumps them to rock bottom.
>
> The pop-ups on our screens or even a half-hour TV broadcast don't give us all the news, just the highlights. (We call 'em highlights even if they're shootings or hurricanes. Nobody covers lowlights.)
>
> We all love mountaintop experiences.
>
> The Greeks envisioned their gods living high on Mount Olympus. The ancients would look to the sky at night and think they were seeing their deities.
>
> A batter hits one out, touches all the bases, and as he crosses the plate, he looks up and points heavenward. Maybe in a post-game interview, he also thanks "the man upstairs."

Something in our lingo, in our thinking, deep inside human beings of every culture and age, senses that up is good, and that good things come from above.

Not *To* Above, For *From* Above . . .!

Mankind's problem is that *we* are always trying to reach what's above. If the good things are up above, we assume, quite naturally, that *we* have to get them—above all, to get ourselves to the place where all good things are. We assume we need to get *to* the things above, rather than having them come down *from* above.

The Greeks knew that no human being could presume to climb Mount Olympus, but people throughout history have always tried to do the next best thing. As early as 3000 BC, the ancient Sumerians and then Babylonians built impressive ziggurats, towers that were essentially stepped pyramids, a large platform with successively smaller platforms stacked on top, reaching high into the sky. The builders believed that the gods lived on top of the ziggurats, and the pagan priests—only the priests—would ascend the steps to provide gifts and offerings to the gods. It may well be that the Tower of Babel (Genesis 11:1-9) was a structure of this kind.

The Aztecs and Mayans in North America, present-day Mexico, likewise built stair-stepped pyramids, often with a temple on top. They believed these would bring them closer to their sun god, moon god, and rain god. In Japanese mythology, beautiful Mount Fuji was seen as the home of a creator goddess or even itself worshiped as a female deity. Pilgrims would climb the mountain in hopes of being reborn, purified, and finding happiness.

This same sort of thinking was a constant temptation to Old Testament Israel. The Canaanites, whom Israel should have eradicated when they entered the Promised Land, worshiped Baal on hilltops, "high places" (Numbers 33:50-52). Baal was a god of rain and fertility—that is, he was believed to bring successful harvests, the crops needed to feed the people. To gain these favors, the Canaanites often worshiped Baal and his consort, the goddess Ashtoreth, with acts of prostitution, as well as child sacrifice. Time and time again, God's people would fall into the trap of imitating these awful practices. The high places were a constant draw to the Israelites for the same idolatries (1 Kings 11:4-7; 2 Kings 17:7-11, 15-17).

Maybe as kids, when we first heard the story of the Tower of Babel, we had this idea: The people wanted to build a "tower with its top in the heavens" (Genesis 11:4)—or even "whose top may reach unto heaven" (King James Version)—so that they could walk up the stairs to get to heaven. Wouldn't have to die and be buried. Just go right now *to* where all those good things are—above. Almost surely, that wasn't really the plan. Even back in those days, they probably knew that wouldn't work.

But in a different sense, the Tower of Babel was intended to get those folks the good things above. "Come, let us build ourselves a city and a tower with its top in the heavens, and let us make a name for ourselves." The city and the great tower—that everyone could see from miles around—would make them famous. They'd all stay together in one place, put the best minds among them to discovering new technologies, set the most skilled carpenters to constructing lavish homes for all, have the ablest farmers grow everyone's dinner, maybe even invent sports by which the fastest, strongest athletes could entertain them. They'd have the best of everything…and they'd accomplish marvelous feats so that future generations would always remember them.

That's how we try to get *to* the things above as well.

And it's very tempting. If the builders of Babel were living the most luxurious lifestyle of their day (just as the Sumerians and Babylonians, the Aztecs and Mayans had the Platinum Mastercards of theirs), well, we, too. And living in luxury, having it all, never satisfies; it only makes us want more.

We want to be famous. Maybe not to every future generation or even the whole world now. But we want to be remembered, not forgotten, when the cool kids are giving out invitations to the party, when Coach decides whom to keep and whom to cut, and when admissions boards are sending out acceptance letters to the school of our choice.

We want the newest technology. Last year's *Madden* doesn't get it this Christmas. We may not care about cleaning up our rooms, but we do want our rooms to be on a street we're not embarrassed about when a friend pulls up in front. (In fact, if she says, "Ooooh," so much the better.) In-N-Out Burger is fine for getting filled up, but for a date, we want to spend quite a bit more to impress—and she probably expects it. We may only be fans—not playing or even playing the video versions—but we want bragging rights over the hated Cowboys or Dodgers and their fans.

Not worth a hill of beans…but we treat them as if they were Mount Everest. Some of those good things up above—that we want to reach up *to* above and grab.

We forget that " every good gift and every perfect gift is *from* above" (James 1:17).

More importantly, we all want to go, eventually, to where the good things are. And by nature, we always try to get ourselves there. Every pagan religion—from the ancient Near East, among the Greeks, Native American—as well as Eastern religions—Shintoism in Japan, Buddhism, Hinduism—and all the western cults, plus pop religion in our own culture ("the man upstairs") all have in common that they try to get us the good things and to their own versions of the good place by our own reaching up. It's the simple logic we all know and experience every day. If you want groceries, you have to pay for them. If you want the boss to pay you, you have to do your work. If you want someone to like you, you have to be nice to them. Makes sense, right? So if we want those good things up above, we have to do what it takes to get in good with that man upstairs.

Won't work. Never does.

We learn the hard way that we can't get *to* what's above, for *from* above we see this: "On the morning of the third day, there were thunders and lightnings and a thick cloud on the mountain and a very loud trumpet blast, so that all the people in the camp trembled. …Now Mount Sinai was wrapped in smoke because the Lord had descended on it in fire. The smoke of it went up like the smoke of a kiln, and the whole mountain trembled greatly. And as the sound of the trumpet grew louder and louder, Moses spoke, and God answered him in thunder. …And God spoke all these words, saying, 'I am the Lord your God, who brought you out of the land of Egypt, out of the house of slavery. You shall have no other gods before Me….' Now when all the people saw the thunder and the flashes of lightning and the sound of the trumpet and the mountain smoking, the people were afraid and trembled, and they stood far off and said to Moses, 'You speak to us, and we will listen; but do not let God speak to us, lest we die'" (Exodus 19:16, 18-19; 20:1-3, 18-19). That's what comes down from above. And you know the other nine Commandments God gave on the same trip down.

So, then, "Who shall ascend the hill of the LORD? And who shall stand in His holy place?" (Psalm 24:3). Who can reach up to the good things above? "He who has clean hands and a pure heart, who does not lift up his soul to what is false" (24:4). That is, anyone who's kept all ten of those Commandments that came down from above—perfectly. Otherwise...not a chance. We only go up in smoke.

Yes, *To* Above, Since *From* Above . . .

This is exactly what Nicodemus knew as he began his famous conversation with Jesus. "Now there was a man of the Pharisees named Nicodemus, a ruler of the Jews. This man came to Jesus by night" (John 3:1-2a). Nicodemus knew those Ten Commandments; the Pharisees were careful students of the law. And he knew that a careful, even perfect, keeping of the law was necessary to ascend to God's presence. Also, as a Pharisee, though, he'd been taught that such a keeping of the law was possible, and that men like himself could, should, would achieve it. Yet, apparently, he sensed something missing. Had he been all that sure of his own obedience to the law, he probably wouldn't have snuck out to see Jesus. Nicodemus was probably sensing just how high that bar of God's holiness, the law of Mount Sinai, really was—as high as the heavens are above the earth!—that he hadn't and never would clear it. He knew what all of our consciences tell us.

That's why the God who truly does dwell in heaven came down from above. To speak to Nicodemus. To lift Nicodemus and every one of his brothers and sisters up to His place above—"who for us men and for our salvation *came down from heaven* and was incarnate by the Holy Spirit of the Virgin Mary and was made man" (Nicene Creed). He who came down from above is the One "who shall ascend the hill of the LORD," "who shall stand in His holy place." And forever change history.

Not every important mountain is as high as Mount Olympus or Mount Fuji or as impossible to "climb" as Mount Sinai. Picture a rocky outcropping, just a hill really, not a mountain, just outside a city we all know. Picture soldiers and steel and blood... *changing history*. Little Round Top it's called, just outside of Gettysburg, Pennsylvania.

On July 2, 1863, Little Round Top was unoccupied—the great Civil War battle already raging nearby—when suddenly it occurred to both Union and Confederate armies that that high ground on the edge of the battlefield might hold the key to ultimate victory or defeat. A small band of Union soldiers arrived at the top just as a much larger Confederate force was charging up the other side. For the next hour, the Union soldiers beat back several Confederate assaults. Finally, down to a few men and out of ammunition, the Union commander, Colonel Chamberlain, ordered his troops to fix bayonets and charge down the hill against one more Confederate attack. The Union counterattack so surprised the Confederates that they surrendered—to a Union force that had no more bullets.

Many historians have concluded that if the Confederates had taken Little Round Top and moved cannons to that high position, they could have forced the Union army to retreat and could have won the Battle of Gettysburg. From there, they could have threatened Washington, D.C., and perhaps pressured President Lincoln to give up the fight against the Confederacy. The South might have won the war, and there would be no United States of America as we know it today.

That would have been a different history. But, of course, we know that's only a small illustration of the other small hill, just outside of Jerusalem, that truly changed the history of the whole human race. Jesus trudged up "Mount" Calvary, entirely unarmed, felt the steel driven by Roman soldiers through his hands and feet, and shed his lifeblood for the sins of the world. Not really a mountain, Calvary, but it towers over heaven and earth. It's the way we get to go to the eternal place above—and the reason we receive every good thing from above right now.

If not for Jesus' death on the high place of Calvary, our sins would forever stand between us and God. Sinful, we could never ascend to the presence of holy God. And with our sin separating us from Him, we could never receive any of the blessings He wishes to shower down on us. But because of Calvary, that's all changed. Sin is gone. Heaven is open. The windows of heaven are open wide, and from them our Father pours down every blessing until they overflow (Malachi 3:10).

Jesus answered Nicodemus, "Truly, truly, I say to you, unless one is born again he cannot see the kingdom of God" (John 3:3). Nicodemus knew the "unless" and "cannot" part. (Remember, that's the part all of us know in our consciences; Mount Sinai is too high for any of us to climb.) Now, Jesus was about to teach Nicodemus how one *can* see the kingdom of God.

Be "born again." How? The Greek text we often translate as "born again" can just as properly be translated "born from above." Being born *from above* is how we can be born again and how we can see the kingdom of God—ascend to that place above, where all good things are and from where all good things come. We know by now that the towers of Babel and the ancients, the mountains of Greece and Japan can't get us to God from below. We can only be reborn from above. But that's what God worked.

"Truly, truly, I say to you," Jesus went on, "unless one is born *of water and the Spirit*, he cannot enter the kingdom of God" (John 3:5). So that's what God did: *re*generated us, made us all over again, with water poured on us as the Holy Spirit came in His Word (Titus 3:5). What Jesus did on the holy high place of Calvary, God now makes personally ours in each of our baptisms. Your sins—personally—forgiven. Every good gift from above given—personally—to you. The promise that, yes, you—personally—will ascend to the place all people long to be forever.

We've all seen images of a baptismal shell dripping down from above. Forget everything we imagine about reaching up to God—towers, mountains, high places. Give up every way we try to grab the good things we sense come only from above. Up is good, but here's how God gives us every truly good thing: Baptism into the high-as-heaven-above event of Christ Jesus on Calvary. Every good gift and every perfect gift *is* from above—personally delivered when God came down from above.

Crucified

Rev. Sam Schuldheisz

Have you ever looked at a work of counted cross-stitch before? Your eyes are first drawn to the scene that is stitched into the fabric canvas. Perhaps the piece is a dish towel full of lighthouses, or a nativity scene stitched into a child's Christmas stocking. Perhaps you have even received a cross-stitch from your mother, grandmother, or friend. Whoever it was that made that piece, and whatever the scene depicted, you can tell that it was made in love, care, compassion, and no doubt, a little blood from a needle prick or two. Cross-stitching is the art of using your hands to make something out of nothing but threads.

But there's something more going on when your eyes look upon a work of cross-stitchery. If you have a piece nearby, take a closer look. Or imagine it this way. At first, you see the scene, object, or animal. Then, as you look closer, you see the individual threads, colors, and one particular shape over and over again. It's the shape that gives this home-craft its name. A little x-shaped cross stitched into the fabric. Once you notice that, you also behold the magnitude of this seemingly simple piece of art. There is not just one cross stitched into the piece, but hundreds and thousands of little crosses all over the towel, cloth, or stocking. There are little crosses everywhere that, when stitched together, tell you a story and show you a picture. And it all starts with a little cross-stitch.

Something like this happens when you open up the story of the Scriptures. You discover God's handiwork. From Genesis to Revelation, God tells you the story of your rescue, redemption, and renewal. God threads His needle with goodness and grace, stitching it all into the people, places, and events of the Scriptures. Scripture is God's cloth upon which He stitches His most important, most beloved work of all: Christ crucified for you. Think of the animal that was sacrificed to cover Adam and Eve's guilt and shame after their sin in Eden. Think of Isaac, who was spared by the sacrifice of a ram in the thicket. Think of the people of Israel saved by the blood of the Passover lamb. Or, think of the tabernacle and the Day of Atonement in Leviticus and the blood of the innocent and holy to cover guilt and unholiness.

When you think about it like that, Scripture is the ultimate work of cross-stitch, where God proclaims His love for us as the hands of Jesus work salvation out of nothing but the dirty rags and threads of our sin. It's God's canvas, where you are knitted and stitched together by the love of Jesus crucified for you.

Opening up Scripture is like looking at those cross-stitched works of art. There's one big picture made of hundreds and thousands of little stitches. One grand story of good news, written by God's grace over and over again in the lives of His people as he brings His work of salvation to completion for you. And there, at the center of it all, is the one cross-stitch that begins, continues, completes, and joins it all together. In the story of the Scriptures, the cross of Jesus is everywhere. It's God's work of art and of amazing grace for you.

What holds all of these things together—the people, places, events, stories, prophets, apostles of the Scriptures, and all baptized believers, and that includes you and me as well? God's promises are bound and woven and threaded together by the greatest cross-stitch of them all: Christ crucified. This is what Paul is getting at when he writes to us all in 1 Corinthians 2:2.

"For I determined to know nothing among you except Jesus Christ, and Him crucified."

What does this mean, that Paul talks only about the crucifixion of Jesus and nothing else in his life or ministry or our faith? No. Not at all. It simply means that Jesus Christ and Him crucified is the center of everything he taught and preached and wrote for the Christian church then and now. Paul was reminding the Corinthians, and he reminds us still today, that whatever it is that we go about doing in our Christian vocations at home, the church, and in the world around us, it's all woven into and out of Jesus Christ and Him crucified.

Thankfully, St. Paul wasn't the last teacher God gave His church to take needle and thread and stitch together God's grace into his teaching and preaching. Centuries later, Martin Luther and the Lutheran Reformation found comfort in the same promise that Paul proclaimed: Jesus Christ and him crucified. Luther put it this way: "Crux sola est nostra theologia." It's a catchy Latin phrase that means, "The cross alone is our theology."

What does this mean? What is Luther telling us? It's the same thing Paul is telling us and the same thing you see in those counted-cross stitch pieces. The cross is everywhere. The hymns we sing, the Scriptures we hear, read, learn, mark, and inwardly digest, the parts of the liturgy we sing and say, the psalms we chant, the prayers we pray, the Gifts of God we receive in water, word, Body and Blood are all cross-stitched together by Jesus Christ and Him crucified. But there's more. In His holy house, with all of His holy Gifts of Baptism, Absolution, the Gospel, and the Supper, Jesus Christ and Him crucified is also cross-stitching you into His life and love.

Jesus Christ and Him crucified threads His needle with Law and Gospel, with grace and goodness, with steadfast love and salvation, and He traces the pattern of His cross over and over again in Divine Service, in your congregation, in your life and faith. You are bound to God's story of Good News by Jesus Christ and Him crucified.

There's a marvelous picture of this in C.S. Lewis's classic story, *The Lion, the Witch, and the Wardrobe*. The magical land of Narnia is stitched together by the sacrifice of Aslan the lion.

"It means," said Aslan, "that though the Witch knew the Deep Magic, there is a magic deeper still which she did not know. Her knowledge goes back only to the dawn of time. But if she could have looked a little further back, into the stillness and the darkness before Time dawned, she would have read there a different incantation. She would

have known that when a willing victim who had committed no treachery was killed in a traitor's stead, the Table would crack and Death itself would start working backward."[1]

As good as the death-destroying work of Aslan is in Narnia, what Jesus does in this world is even better, because it truly happened. In Narnia, Aslan's sacrifice does for Lucy, Edmund, Susan, Peter, and all of Narnia what Jesus Christ and him crucified does for us all in this world. Jesus, the Lion of Judah, goes to the cross. Jesus is our willing victim and priest and mediator all at once. Jesus is the one who committed no treachery, and yet, He who knew no sin became sin for us (2 Corinthians 5:21). Jesus is the one who is killed in the traitor's stead—that's you and me, traitors turned into children of God. Jesus is the one crucified for you, risen for you, the one who cracks the stone table of the grave wide open for you, and carries you on His back out alive again.

This is why the cross alone is our theology. Unlike the world around us, Jesus Christ and him crucified is steady. Stable. Steady. Steadfast. Firm. Faithful. Christ crucified is our anchor in the storm. Our mighty fortress from the enemy. Our trusty shield and weapon against the old evil foe. In the words of the Cistercian monks, *stat crux dum volvitur orbis.* "The cross stands firm while the world turns."

There are many moments, minutes, hours, days, weeks, months, even years of our lives that seem wobbly, shaky, chaotic, wind-tossed, and storm-driven. We have days, and sometimes long nights, of darkness, despair, doubt, grief, guilt, shame, sorrow, and hopelessness. All too often, we feel as if we're standing on shifting sands, as if life itself is coming unraveled one thread at a time. Days when the devil, the world, and our sinful flesh cause us to come apart at the seams, to be undone and ensnared in a thousand knots of iniquities. For all the times you have moments, minutes, days, hours, weeks, months, and years like that, God has cross-stitched his promise across the pages of Holy Scripture for you.

Your life at some point, perhaps even now, might feel like a complete tangled mess of bare threads, but fear not. The great Artist of amazing grace is with you. You are His handiwork. And you are

---

[1] C.S. Lewis, *The Chronicles of Narnia. The Lion, the Witch, and the Wardrobe.* New York: Harper Collins Publishers, 2001, p. 185.

bound to and cross-stitched into the one who was pierced, not with needles and threads, but with nails and a spear for you and for all those dark, lonely, sinful days. Jesus Christ and Him crucified sows his word and promise into your ears, hearts, and minds. You might feel like you're losing your grip, on your last thread, but Christ holds fast.

And that's not all. Jesus Christ and Him crucified is the light in the darkness. As another Latin phrase goes, *Christi crux est mihi lux.* "The cross of Christ is light to me."

Jesus Christ is the light of the world, the light no darkness, even the darkness of Good Friday, can overcome. When Joseph languished in the pit and later in prison, in the dark, forgotten by the world, God remembered Joseph and raised him up to the right hand of Pharaoh. He provided for many. He gave outrageous forgiveness to his undeserving brothers. When Jonah was in the dark, dank, and disgusting belly of the fish for three days and three nights, God remembered him and commanded the fish to spit him out again on dry land. When David mourned and grieved his sin and shame with Bathsheba, God remembered him and delivered him a promise. Out of the darkness of King David's sin would come one who is David's son yet David's Lord, the King of kings and Lord of lords. The Light of the world. Jesus Christ and him crucified.

When you find yourself walking in the dark valley of the shadow of death, the same Lord who was with Joseph, Jonah, and David is with you. The cross of Jesus Christ and Him crucified is light and life and love, deep and wide and big enough to swallow all the darkness and shine with light undying. You are cross-stitched into Jesus Christ and him crucified. Your foundation. Your anchor. Your light.

The Cross of Christ is Light to me
In death's dark vale and misery.
E'en though we walk through deepest night
Christ crucified will be our light.

When filled with fear and tossed about,
When stormed by gales of gloom and doubt,
When weeping tarries through the night,
The cross of Christ will be your light.

And though the world around us turns
The love of Christ will ne'er adjourn.
Christ's word, a lamp, our life, and guide
His cross forever will abide.

Oh cross of Christ, still lead us on
Until our final rest is won.
Come quickly, Jesus, Lord we pray
And bring us to the endless day.

All glory, thanks, and praise be sung
Unto the Father, Spirit, Son.
For now and all eternity,
The cross of Christ is light to me.

The Cross of Christ is Light to Me
Tune O WALY WALY (see Lutheran Service Book, hymn 595)
Sam Schuldheisz (2020, February 2—The Purification of Mary and Presentation of Our Lord)

The Weight of Praise

Rev. Donavon Riley

> *"I will praise the Lord all my life; I will sing praise to my God as long as I live."*—Psalm 146:2

The words have been sung for over a thousand years. *Te Deum laudamus.* We praise You, O God. Not in the light, easy way that words of praise often slip from the tongue, but with a gravity that bends the spine, with the weight of centuries pressing through the syllables. This is no ordinary hymn; it is an act of endurance, a standing up under the full burden of God's presence, of history, of the unfathomable truth that He is and has always been.

To say *Te Deum* is to step into a tradition that stretches beyond memory. The hymn's origins are cloaked in legend—some say it was composed by Saint Ambrose and Saint Augustine in a moment of divine inspiration at Augustine's Baptism. Others trace it back to Nicetas of Remesiana, a lesser-known but weighty figure in the early church. Regardless of its precise beginnings, *Te Deum* emerged from an era when words were costly, when faith was a fire that had to be guarded, when the Christian life was anything but comfortable. It was a hymn for men who knew the hard weight of belief, who bore their faith in their bodies as well as their souls.

It has been sung in coronations and battlefields, in the triumphs of kings and the dirges of the fallen. It was chanted when Clovis was baptized in the waters of a Frankish river, when Charlemagne was crowned emperor, and when the first stones of Christendom's great churches were set into the earth. But it is not a hymn of the high and mighty alone. It belongs just as much to the unseen hands that tilled the land, to the voices that never made history but made the faith endure, who sang it without fanfare in parish churches and candlelit chapels. It was lifted by pilgrims on the long road, by monks bent over their breviaries in cold stone cloisters, by priests saying their last Mass before the executioner's blade. It was carried on the tongues of the faithful, who clung to it not as ornament but as armor.

The old monks knew what they were saying when they first chanted it in the hush of early morning, when breath and candlelight and Latin mingled in the cold air. The words do not waver, do not leave room for half-hearted devotion. They rise with the certainty of stone laid upon stone, the slow building of cathedrals, of hands that have shaped the faith from martyr's blood and farmer's toil alike. They are not polite. They are not safe. They do not just thank—they acclaim, they proclaim, they declare before heaven and earth what cannot be ignored: *Sanctus, sanctus, sanctus—holy, holy, holy!* They summon the whole of creation to bear witness to the truth that does not change.

And at the center of that truth stands Christ. His name does not appear in the opening lines, but He is there, the axis around which all true praise must turn. The *Te Deum* does not praise an unknown God. It exalts the God who has walked among us, who has taken on flesh, who has borne our sorrows.

Midway through the hymn, the words sharpen into focus: *Tu Rex gloriae, Christe—You are the King of Glory, O Christ.* The King of Glory who is crowned, not in gold, but in thorns. He reigns, not from a throne, but from a cross. And still, the church sings: *Tu Rex gloriae, Christe.* This is where all praise must arrive, at the name that is above every name, the name before which every knee shall bow. Christ is not an afterthought in this hymn. He is the reason it can be sung at all. Without Him, there is no bridge between earth and heaven, no lifting of human voices that can reach the throne of God. Without Him, even the purest praise would be a song sung into the void. But in Him, our words are caught up into something greater than ourselves. Our voices, weak as they are, join in the chorus of saints and angels, the unending praise of the church triumphant.

And that is the great wonder of it. The *Te Deum* is not a hymn for the strong, for those sure of their place in history. It is a hymn for the weary, the battle-worn, the ones who have fought and failed and risen again. It is for the farmer in his fields, the mother at her hearth, the old man kneeling in a darkened chapel. It is for those who know that life does not always feel like victory, but who praise nonetheless, because they know that victory has already been won. The words endure because the faith endures. The song does not end.

But what does it mean to praise in such a way? To say *Te Deum* is not to offer up something smooth, something polished to fit the world's tastes, something harmless and well-mannered. It is not a song that asks permission to be sung. It is a battle cry, a defense against despair, a declaration that God reigns regardless of the shifting tides of history. It is praise with muscle in it, praise that does not come cheaply. It does not murmur agreement with the world; it stands against it, unyielding.

We do not say *Te Deum* because we feel like it, because life is comfortable, because our days have been free of suffering. The words are not shaped by how the wind blows, by whether fortune has been kind or cruel. We say it because *God is who He is*, and His reign does not flicker with the passing of seasons, does not bow to the rise and fall of empires, and does not grow dim when the night lengthens. The saints and martyrs who have gone before us knew this. They sang it in chains, in prison cells, in the silence of catacombs, in times when the faith itself was outlawed. They lifted it up when the flames licked at their feet, when swords were drawn against them, and when exile, torture, and death were their reward.

The hymn holds in it the iron will of those who refused to bow to lesser gods. It is the song of those who stood before kings and said, *We will not serve your idols.* It is the voice of those who went to the scaffold with prayers on their lips, the last cry of those who would rather die with Christ than live without Him. To praise in such a way is not a sentimental act but a *holy insistence*—that He is worthy, even when the world shakes, even when everything else crumbles, even when the night seems endless.

In this, *Te Deum* is an act of resistance. It stands against the softening of faith, the slow erosion of conviction, the temptation to make God a private comfort rather than the Lord of history. It does not bend, does not flatter, does not negotiate with the world's whims. It is sung in defiance of every force that would shrink God down, that would make Him small, manageable, something easy to carry. But He is not small. He is not a god of compromise. He is the Alpha and the Omega, the fire at the heart of all things, the One before whom the nations are dust.

To sing *Te Deum* is to acknowledge this—not with fear, but with awe. It is to know that our voices, frail as they are, join in the chorus of heaven, that when we take up the words, we are standing in the company of saints and angels, in the presence of the One whose glory does not fade.

There is something raw about its language, something unfiltered. It does not ask for understanding—it *commands* it. It does not ask for agreement—it *states* the reality of God's glory as a fact beyond argument. It is the sound of the church standing firm, unshaken, while the world tries to reshape itself again and again.

And what of today? What does it mean to sing *Te Deum* in an age where so much has been flattened, where even faith is treated as just another personal preference, another lifestyle choice? To praise God in this way now is to resist the temptation to make Him smaller, to make our faith merely private, mild, and unobtrusive.

But faith is never mild. The words *Te Deum laudamus* still ring out, and they are as dangerous as they ever were. To say them with meaning is to throw our lot in with something ancient and unyielding, something that does not bend to modern whim. It is to recognize that holiness is not a comfortable thing, that the presence of God is not a soft glow but a purging fire.

In a world that dismisses the sacred, *Te Deum* remains a challenge. It asks if we truly believe that God reigns, if we truly trust that He is who He says He is. And if we do, then our praise cannot be shallow. It cannot be conditional. It must be full-throated, fearless, and unafraid of what it means to acknowledge a God who demands everything of us.

And so the hymn continues. It is sung in cathedrals and chapels, in monasteries and mission fields, in places where faith is celebrated and in places where it is barely tolerated. It is sung in sickness and in health, in peace and in war, in times of certainty and in times of doubt. And wherever it is sung, Christ is present. The words belong to Him. The praise rises to Him.

This is the song of the church, the song of those who know that heaven is not empty, that God is not absent, and that Christ has already won the victory. It is the hymn of those who have seen the world's power fade and crumble but know that His kingdom does not end. *Te Deum laudamus.*

The words are still sung. And they will be sung until the day when faith gives way to sight, when every knee bows, when the praise we offer in hope becomes the praise of those who see His glory face to face.

Bread of Life

Rev. Duane Bamsch

> *Jesus said to them, "I am the bread of life; whoever comes to me shall not hunger, and whoever believes in me shall never thirst."* —John 6:35

When you think of the Bread of Life, this is likely the biblical text that comes to mind. These are the words Jesus says following the feeding of the five thousand. But in order to fully understand what Jesus says about Himself, and who He is for you, one must look at *all* of Holy Scripture, for as St. Irenaeus said, "All of the Scriptures are a mosaic that reveal the image and icon of Christ." That is, the Bible is a collection of the individual pieces of a mosaic that fit together to make the whole image (or icon) of Christ that is given to us. All of God's Word taken together shows us Jesus. One must look at *all* of Holy Scripture to see the full picture and context. You can't use just *one* word, *one* verse, or *one* chapter standing alone as the deciding factor for what you believe without looking at the whole of Holy Scripture.

In order to see how foundational this claim of Jesus as the Bread of Life is, you have to go all the way back to the Book of Exodus. The Israelites have fled Egypt under God's protection, and they are deep in the wilderness, far from the fertile lands that produced so much of their food while they were in captivity. How will they stay alive out here, surrounded by rocks, scrub, sand, and...not much else? How will they make for themselves bread to live? And in that question is the reminder that they aren't properly thinking this through. The Lord God Almighty has brought them out of Egypt, out of the land of slavery by the might of His outstretched arm, preserving them from death, and they are complaining about where *they* will find food.

They have been magnificently and gloriously delivered from the death of captivity, and they are already installing themselves as "god." There hasn't even been time to get their catechisms printed, and they are already abandoning their Lord and God! "Where will *we* find food?" they ask, already turning to their own power rather than trusting the God who delivered them. And yet, in His infinite mercy, Almighty God sends them manna, literal bread from heaven, to sustain and strengthen them. And He provides this heavenly food each and every day until the Children of Israel cross the Jordan River into the Promised Land, more than forty years in the future.

Why does He do this? Why does God lead His people kicking and screaming from Egypt, where they seem to think life is just fine? Because it was God's will to save his people and return them to the land He had promised to Abraham, so that His Messiah would come to fulfill all of the sacrifices and promises of old. Yes, saving you eternally was the ultimate goal of rescuing His people from Egypt. He led them out so that He could send the Word in the flesh to 'tabernacle' among His people. God's will to save you is 'enfleshed,' as it were, so that the life of Christ himself would be your salvation.

Centuries after the wilderness wanderings and the giving of daily bread to the Children of Israel, and the offerings of sacrifices in both tabernacle and temple, Jesus associates Himself with this manna, the bread that is given. He says the words above in response to those who looked for an easy solution, an easy path to the kingdom; an easy meal, in other words. Those who questioned Him saw Moses as the giver of the manna, not God. Jesus has to remind them from whom all these Gifts ultimately come. They aren't given by Moses or the prophets; they are given by God Himself. So, ultimately, Jesus is the one who sustains all of His people, no matter what their wilderness wanderings in this world look like. He freely and continuously gives what is needed for their, for our, and for all Christian's lives in this world. But to understand that, you also need to look at this miraculous feeding of the five thousand through the lens of Psalm 23.

In the same way that the Shepherd-King makes David and all believers lie down in the green pastures of the psalm to receive all that he has to give, Jesus tells His hungry listeners to sit down and rest in the bountiful grass (there was "much grass in the place," St. John says). There, in peace and safety (beside the still waters of the Sea of Galilee?) Jesus sets a table that overflows with abundance. It is a peek into the future for all who trust in Him, for all to whom the Holy Spirit gives faith. A prelude to the Lord's Supper and of the eternal feast promised by Isaiah and so many others. Thousands upon thousands of hungry people eat their fill of bread and fish, which had been miraculously multiplied by Jesus from one boy's lunch, and even then, twelve baskets full of bread are gathered up afterwards. So much bread was given that they couldn't possibly consume it all.

Why are the remnants and leftovers gathered up? So that they would not perish. That's the force of the Greek text here. This abundant, life-giving bread should not perish. Unlike the manna of the wilderness—which lasted only the day and then spoiled—this bread, given by the Bread of Life, should not perish, but remain to give its Gift of life and sustenance another day.

And that verse, that word (perish), sends you back a few chapters in St. John's Gospel. To chapter three, where Jesus explains to Nicodemus that He has been sent by the Father so that no one who believes in Him would perish but have everlasting life. How does one not perish? By ingesting that which does not perish, the very Bread of Life given for you. Because Jesus is the bread that gives a life that is not merely physical and doomed to perish but preserves eternally. And that bread is given to you in so many ways.

It is important to remember that the disciples gathered up *twelve* baskets of bread. Essentially, one for each disciple to carry in his vocation as apostle. Each of them takes up that which doesn't perish to give it to those hungry and thirsty for righteousness. Just as your pastor delivers the Bread of Life to you to this day! Of course, the form of that bread—whether Jesus speaks of the Lord's Supper or of faith—has been a topic of debate for centuries, but it doesn't have to be so hard to understand. Simply put, the Father gives the Son, who is the true bread from heaven (anticipated by the manna of the exodus), to those who gladly receive and rejoice in it. That means that Jesus is, in Himself, the very substance and content of eternal life; he is the very *incarnation* of eternal life, he *embodies* eternal life for you, and everything he gives contains that eternal life—from His taking on of our flesh, to his own Baptism in the Jordan river, the words of His mouth, the miracles of His hands, the Eucharist, his death and resurrection, and his promised return on the Last Day.

To fully grasp how such a simple phrase ("I am the bread of life") can mean something so overwhelming and magnificent, one must go back into the Old Testament again, to Deuteronomy chapter 8, where Moses reminds the gathered Children of Israel that they did not live on manna alone in their wilderness wanderings. Rather, they lived on "every word that [came] from the mouth of the Lord." As hard as they tried, it wasn't all about them. As much as they thought they had soldiered on and conquered adversity from the Red Sea to the banks of the Jordan River on their own power, they truly didn't do anything to sustain themselves and work toward the goal of the Promised Land; it was all (and only) the grace and Gift of God in His Word that had gotten them that far. All of it was Almighty God working to prepare a place for His children until the time had fully come for the Son of God to fulfill the promise made to Adam and Eve after the Fall.

There is yet one more trip through Holy Scripture for us concerning this bread, which comes down from heaven. Look back to how Jesus gives this bread to the gathered thousands. He takes the bread, He gives thanks, and then He distributes it to those around Him. Reading these words, you hear the other Gospels and what they say about the institution of the Lord's Supper. The phrasing is so similar. And that phrasing also takes you to Luke 24, where the risen Jesus does almost the same thing at the table in Emmaus. He took their bread, blessed it, broke it, and gave it to them. And in that action, the two men there recognized their Lord, the Bread of Life! All of these texts point to the same conclusion: Jesus, the risen Christ, is the true Bread of Life come down from above for you and your salvation.

The thing to remember about St. John is that he writes his Gospel to reveal Jesus *sacramentally*. Jesus is the one who is received by faith and the one received by mouth as the Savior. All four of the Gospels that we have been given were written not as day-to-day diaries about a series of events, but instead to teach us the faith. To teach us about Jesus. To speak—with the living Word of God—faith into our ears, minds, and hearts. To instill within us a hunger and a thirst for the Bread of Life, which comes down from heaven and gives life to the world.

This gives comfort to the Christian today. Since Jesus is the Bread of Life, we can rest in Him, knowing that our struggles don't gain life everlasting for us. Our difficulties in this life do not 'promote' us to the Kingdom of God. Striving and reaching and trying to grasp that which God the Father gives does not do us any good eternally. Yes, those things form a discipline and a pattern of service within each of us. And that enables us to live in a way in which our love for God is shown to our neighbors, but there is no earning a place at the table of the eternal wedding feast of the Lamb in his kingdom. There is only receiving that which is given.

There is only following the Shepherd-King where he leads and resting near the still waters of Baptism, reclining in the green pastures of his abundant Word, and receiving that which He gives abundantly: overflowing Gifts of forgiveness, life, and salvation, which are poured out of the overflowing cup of His presence among us upon His altar and in His church. This is how Almighty God provides the Bread of Life through all of our wilderness wandering until we enter the Promised Land of the New Creation and the marriage feast of the Lamb, which has no end. So then, receiving the Supper, the Eucharist, is receiving the Body and Blood of the Christ. Both in faith, by hearing the very Word of God, and in the act of tasting and seeing that the Lord is good. We pray that the Lord would "give us this day our daily bread," and he does that, faithfully and continually. That daily bread is the Word made flesh. The Word of God takes tangible form in the Supper. The Word made flesh is the Bread of Life, given for you!

Here I Stand

Rev. Chris Hull

On April 17th, 1521, Dr. Martin Luther, of blessed and holy memory, was asked a question. He was brought to Worms to answer for his teachings and the movements that they had caused. Luther was examined and called to recant his writings because they contradicted the edicts of the Pope. Luther was asked to recant and stop teaching. Luther requested a day to meditate on this heavy demand in order that he, a Doctor of Theology, could answer clearly and rightly.

On April 18th, Luther was again asked by the papal legate to recant his writings, and he responded in German with a plethora of reasons why he could not recant his writings as a whole, but could recant those times that he wrote against individuals with harshness. When done speaking, the Emperor, Charles V, asked Luther to say the same thing again, but in Latin, Luther summed up his speech, saying:

> Since your most serene majesty and your highnesses require of me a simple, clear, and direct answer, I will give one, and it is this: I cannot

> submit my faith either to the pope or to the council, because it is clear that they have fallen into error and even into inconsistency with themselves. If, then, I am not convinced by proof from Holy Scripture, or by cogent reasons, if I am not satisfied by the very text I have cited, and if my judgment is not in this way brought into subjection to God's word, I neither can nor will retract anything; for it cannot be either safe or honest for a Christian to speak against his conscience. Here I stand. I cannot do otherwise. God help me. Amen.[1]

Luther's faith could not be submitted to the will of the pope, a church council, or anything that is corrupted by fallen reason and senses. Faith submits to Christ Jesus alone, to the Word of God alone. As the church sings in her song, "Faith clings to Jesus' cross alone, and rests in Him unceasing."[2] Luther stood, not on his works, nor the will of any man, but on the Word of God alone. This is what it means to confess, "Here I stand. I cannot do otherwise. God help me. Amen." Luther's faith and our faith are not built upon the feebleness of fallen works, reason, and emotion, but rather stand on the blood, wounds, and death of our Lord and Savior Jesus Christ, and the means by and through which the Gifts of His death and resurrection are given to us.

Faith does not stand on the feebleness of fallen works, reason, and emotion. The object of faith is not our works, for they cannot nor do not gain salvation, as the church bellows forth Luther's hymn singing, "Our works cannot salvation gain, they merit only endless pain."[3] Works cannot gain salvation because there is not one work that trumps our sinful condition. Only the blood, wounds, and death of Jesus Christ merit salvation for us. As the Catechism says concerning the 2nd article of the Creed, that Jesus did not purchase and win us with silver and gold, but "with His holy and precious blood, and with His innocent suffering and death." Only the good work that Jesus finished on the cross for us gains us salvation, deliverance from sin, death, the world, and the power of the devil.

---

[1] Roland Bainton, *Here I Stand: A Life of Martin Luther* (Nashville: Abingdon Press, 1978), 181-182.

[2] *Lutheran Service Book*, 555.9.

[3] *Lutheran Service Book*, 581.12.

Faith does not stand on corrupted reason. What does this mean? It means that we do not receive comfort from that which makes sense to our fallen logic and thinking. The assurance of our salvation is not dependent on our reason and senses but instead depends on the solid ground of God's Word. Luther did not draw comfort from how he experienced God but was comforted in God's Word to him. Luther suffered in his attempt to be good enough to appease the wrath of God. However, no matter how many good works he performed or how many sins he confessed, he could not rest in the assurance of his salvation. However, in the late 1510s, Luther was given the mercy of God as he studied Scripture and heard the gospel through his father confessor, Johann Staupitz. Bainton summarizes this gospel experience in his biography of Luther, saying:

> A new view also of God is here. The All Terrible is the All Merciful too. Wrath and love fuse upon the cross. The hideousness of sin cannot be denied or forgotten; but God, who desires not that a sinner should die but that he should turn and live, has found the reconciliation in the pangs of bitter death. It is not that the Son by his sacrifice has placated the irate Father; it is not primarily that the Master by his self-abandoning goodness had made up for our deficiency. It is that in some inexplicable way, in the utter desolation of the forsaken Christ, God was able to reconcile the world to himself......Who can understand this? Philosophy is unequal to it. Only faith can grasp so high a mystery.[4]

Luther studied, as a professor of theology, Galatians, the Psalms, Romans, and the rest of Scripture, and in this God showed Himself to Luther that he may know and stand, not on his own works, but on the mercy of God in Christ Jesus alone. Luther stood, not on his work, not on his experience and reasoning, but on the rock-solid Word of God that reveals, not a god of wrath, but the One True God of mercy and grace.

Faith does not stand on the shallowness of human emotion. Luther experienced feeling hated by God, as if God could never love him because of his sin. Rather than trusting those emotions, Luther

---

[4] Bainton, *Here I Stand*, 48-49.

was graced to receive the Word of God that pointed him to the cross, where the full pardon and remission of his sins stands purchased and won. This truth is not self-evident, nor something that one experiences outside of the Word. Luther made this clear in his confession, the Smalcald Articles, in 1537. Here, when writing on confession, Luther makes the point that God does not deal with us except by His external Word when critiquing Enthusiasm, saying:

> In short, enthusiasm clings to Adam and his descendants from the beginning to the end of the world. It is a poison implanted and inoculated in man by the old dragon, and it is the source, strength, and power of all heresy, including that of the papacy and Mohammedanism. Accordingly, we should and must constantly maintain that God will not deal with us except through his external Word and sacrament. Whatever is attributed to the Spirit apart from such Word and sacrament is of the devil.[5]

The enthusiast yearns to have an inner experience, an emotional awakening that solidifies his or her deliverance from sin, death, the world, and the power of the devil. The enthusiast, in short, seeks God and to know God outside of His Word. What did Luther say about this? He said that it is of the devil. Whenever one stands on their inner experience or emotions to rest their faith, the devil is quick to sweep the rug from underneath their feet. Luther did not stand on his emotions but instead stood on the firm ground of God's Word that never changes.

On April 18th, 1521, Luther stood on the Word of God and prayed for God to help him. He did this because he knew, through the Word of God working on him, that he could not rely on the shifting ground of works, reason, and emotion. We know why he said it. He confessed these words because faith clings not to our work, but to the finished work of Christ the crucified. Luther's voice bellowed forth the truth that man is saved, not by meriting God's favor via his own works, but by trusting that Jesus has accomplished salvation for him by His blood, wounds, and death. We know why Luther said this. It

[5] Smalcald Articles, VIII.9-10, Tappert, 313.

is also important, maybe even necessary, to know to whom Luther said this.

To whom did Luther say, 'Here I stand?" He did not whisper these words to his Father Confessor. He did not quietly talk about these words with like-minded friends over dinner. Luther did not say these words to his students, who were bound to listen to him because their future depended on it. To whom did Luther say these powerful, life-changing, soul-reviving words? You could say that he said these words to Charles V. You could say he said these words to the papal legate and therefore to the pope himself. You could say he spoke these words before the nobility of the Holy Roman Empire. You could say that he bellowed these words to the people of Germany, that they could be freed from the darkness of the papacy. And, if you guessed these groups, you would be partially correct. However, Luther said these words, nay, confessed these words to His Lord and Savior, Jesus Christ, and to the whole host of heaven. Luther spoke these words before God, Father, Son, and Holy Spirit Himself. Luther spoke these words unto eternity as a struggling saint dependent on God's mercy to rescue him and carry him unto life everlasting.

Luther confessed these words before the whole company of heaven. He confessed, "Here I Stand," before his Lord Jesus, despairing of himself, and relying completely on Jesus for his salvation. Is this not the same for every Christian today, or at least it should be? These words, though spoken by Luther, are the words of the faithful. The faithful does not stand on his or her works, reason, or emotions, but instead stands on the mercy of God in Christ Jesus alone. These words are then spoken to the whole company of heaven, and to the church throughout the ages. The church still stands, not on Her works, reason, or emotions, but on the Word of God. It is the Word that still remains as we sing in our hymn.

Here I stand, said Luther. Here I stand, says the church. May all the faithful then continue to confess these words, knowing that they stand on the firm ground that never wavers or shakes. May the Holy Spirit continue to bless the church that She may continue to be filled with little Luthers who confess the truth that we are saved not by works, but by faith in Jesus Christ alone. Amen.

Sanctified

Rev. Richard Heinz

"You shall be holy, for I the LORD your God am holy" (Leviticus 19:2). God declares this truth to His Old Testament church, and it continues to be as He declared. God's Word does what it says. He says you shall be holy, and you are. But our Lutheran minds ask, "What does this mean?" What is "holy?" What causes it? And how and when are our lives holy?

The Latin word *sanctus* simply means "holy." So "sanctify" is the English verb form that comes from *sanctus*: "to make holy."

What is "Holy?"

To be holy is to be set apart; unlike anything or anyone in this common, broken, spiritually polluted world. At creation, the LORD God made a perfect world, with Adam and Eve as the crown of His perfect and holy creation. Without sin, everything was good and reflecting His goodness and glory. Man and Woman lived in a righteous, loving, and perfect relationship with the Lord and each other. This was a holy life.

When Eve and Adam rebelled and fell, that holiness was shattered. All creation fell with them into a broken existence, vulgar and outside of that perfect relationship that was. The perfect fellowship with our holy God was shattered.

That's why, several thousand years later, the Prophet Isaiah thought he was doomed when, in a vision, he was brought into the throne room of the LORD of hosts; in his common, unclean flesh, he was sure that he'd be destroyed simply by being in the perfect holy presence of God.

"In the year that King Uzziah died I saw the Lord sitting upon a throne, high and lifted up; and the train of his robe filled the temple. Above him stood the seraphim. Each had six wings: with two he covered his face, and with two he covered his feet, and with two he flew. And one called to another and said:

'Holy, holy, holy is the Lord of hosts; the whole earth is full of his glory!' And the foundations of the thresholds shook at the voice of him who called, and the house was filled with smoke. And I said: 'Woe is me! For I am lost; for I am a man of unclean lips, and I dwell in the midst of a people of unclean lips; for my eyes have seen the King, the Lord of hosts!'" (Isaiah 6:1-5)

Even the holy angels were averting their eyes, hiding their faces in awe and humility. Yet Isaiah was there to see it all. The smoke of incense. The shaking of the Temple itself at this holy presence of God. It was overwhelming.

"Then one of the seraphim flew to me, having in his hand a burning coal that he had taken with tongs from the altar. And he touched my mouth and said: 'Behold, this has touched your lips; your guilt is taken away, and your sin atoned for'" (Isaiah 6:6-7).

Isaiah could not stand in God's presence by being holy in and of himself. He stood having been made holy by God, through means that He gave.

You Are Made Holy

What does it mean to be made holy, to be sanctified? Perhaps it could be understood through the familiar words of Luther's Post-Communion Collect: "in faith toward You and in fervent love toward one another." The loving of one's neighbor flows from the holiness given by God and received in faith. The works of love for your neighbor are readily seen fruits of faith and evidence of sanctification.

"Who Makes You Holy?" seems to be a topic that divides many Christians, even if they don't realize it. Virtually every Christian will agree that it starts with God. *"For this is the will of God, your sanctification"* (1 Thessalonians 4:3). The Lord desires us to be holy, set apart from the sin and brokenness of this world. However, how this happens and "who is the doer of the verbs" will be what divides us from here.

Many will say that we cooperate with God. He gets the ball rolling with our sanctification, and we have to go along with it. We "do our part" and work with Him. This idea is common to our friends in the Roman Church and many Protestants. They may differ on explaining it, but in the end, some portion of your sanctification was done by God, and some portion is due to your own work with Him.

The problem with that? It is not what God's Word says. The Lord does not describe your holiness as your own doing, even if only a tiny percentage of your own doing. He can't be any clearer than when He declared to Moses: *"I am the LORD who sanctifies you"* (Leviticus 22:32).

What Makes You Holy?

Word

St. Paul reminds us that a thing in creation *"is made holy by the word of God and prayer"* (1 Timothy 4:5). Not that our own prayer makes it so, but that prayer responds to the Word of God proclaimed and heard among us.

The night that Jesus celebrated His Last Supper with the Apostles, and instituted His Holy Supper, He taught much and prayed: *"Sanctify them in the truth; your word is truth"* (John 17:17). The Word of God IS the very truth that makes us holy. His Word does what it says; when the Lord declares us to be holy in His Word, He grants that to be.

Baptism

We are blessed as Lutherans to recognize the real and beautiful Gift of this new birth from above (John 3). Not simply a moment of deciding for Christ, or pledging allegiance to our Savior, Baptism is a work of God, washing you into forgiveness, rescue, and salvation. Just as these Gifts are His work and not yours, so also is the Gift of holiness. The Lord sets you apart, "being separated from the multitude of unbelievers and serving [God's] name" (LSB p. 269, Rite of Holy Baptism).

But you were washed, you were sanctified, you were justified in the name of the Lord Jesus Christ and by the Spirit of God (1 Corinthians 6:11). This precious Sacrament delivers God's gracious and forgiving Gifts, with faith to receive His justification. This, in turn, begins a life of being set apart and serving one's neighbor with the works God has prepared for you.

Absolution

This is one that modern Lutherans tend to overlook or forget. And yet, it is a sweet and precious Gift given to the church on that first Easter evening.

So Jesus said to them again, "Peace to you! As the Father has sent Me, I also send you." And when He had said this, He breathed on them, and said to them, "Receive the Holy Spirit. If you forgive the sins of any, they are forgiven them; if you retain the sins of any, they are retained" (John 20:21-23 NKJV).

Jesus breathes the Holy Spirit on the apostles. He uses this strange but simple action to send them, that they may give His holiness, along with the forgiveness delivered through His Gifts.

Eucharist

"Whoever feeds on my flesh and drinks my blood abides in me, and I in him" (John 6:56).

Think about it. If your holy Lord abides in you, He is making you holy from within. If you are eating nutritious food, it is giving you strength and nourishment. It is building you into a healthy human being. How much more, when the holy and precious Body and Blood of Christ are being fed to you in the Holy Supper? Christ enters you, feeds and sustains you, nourishes you with Himself! He is transforming you from within.

The main thing about the blessed Sacrament of the Altar is not that we are doing this in remembrance of Him, or that the pastor is offering some service to God, but that your Holy, Holy, Holy Lord God comes to you in His Body and Blood, veiled in bread and wine, *given and shed for you.*

When Are You Holy?

Next comes the question: When are you holy?

Old Adam was drowned at Baptism, and yet, he's a strong swimmer. He keeps coming to the surface and gasping for breath, trying to pull you under. That is often misunderstood by so many. Other Christians will describe sanctification as if you could see this gradually climbing line on a graph. It seems to imply that holiness just keeps getting better throughout life if you are a real Christian, believe hard enough, and are sincere enough. But that is not what the Bible teaches.

The Small Catechism reminds us that Baptism *"indicates that the Old Adam in us should by daily contrition and repentance be drowned and die with all sins and evil desires, and that a new man should daily emerge and arise to live before God in righteousness and purity forever."*

"We were therefore buried with Him through baptism into death in order that, just as Christ was raised from the dead through the glory of the Father, we too may live a new life" (Romans 6:4). That means always, every day, you are to begin anew and live the holy life that goes hand in hand with your identity as God's Child – an identity given to you in Holy Baptism. You constantly fail, as the Catechism reminds us in the Fifth Petition of the Lord's Prayer: *"we daily sin much."* Yet our good and gracious God brings us to repentance and gives His forgiveness, gifting us with holiness again.

Just because you daily sin much does not mean that you are an imposter. You are an authentic Christian, a child of God through water and the Word. God did not make a mistake in making you His child. Even if there are lapses in your holiness, Christ still sets you apart from the world as His own, constantly *"[calling] you out of darkness into his marvelous light"* (1 Peter 2:9).

What does this mean?

For we are his workmanship, created in Christ Jesus for good works, which God prepared beforehand, that we should walk in them (Ephesians 2:10). You have been created, and through the death and resurrection of Christ, with benefits delivered in Word and Sacrament, recreated as God's holy child. As His child, He blesses you with works of love, that you may serve your neighbor in holiness. Will that be perfect and constant? As long as you dwell in this fallen existence, no. But Christ Jesus has gathered you into His bride, the church. He *"gave himself up for her, that he might sanctify her, having cleansed her by the washing of water with the word, so that he might present the church to himself in splendor, without spot or wrinkle or any such thing, that she might be holy and without blemish"* (Ephesians 5:25-27).

You are forgiven, cleansed, and sanctified in splendor! Rejoice, dear Child of God; Jesus sends His Spirit to make you holy, that you *may be His own and live under Him in His kingdom and serve Him in everlasting righteousness, innocence, and blessedness, just as He is risen from the dead, lives and reigns to all eternity. This is most certainly true* (Small Catechism: Creed: 2nd Article).

Concordia

Rev. Joel Fritsche

Concordia! For Lutherans, this is not an unfamiliar word. Lutheran churches, universities, seminaries, and institutions bear this name, as does the official publishing house of the Lutheran Church—Missouri Synod (LCMS). Our Lutheran Confessions bear the name "Concordia," or similarly, "The Book of Concord." Indeed, "Concordia" is a word of importance for Lutherans, certainly from the time of the Reformation to the present day and beyond. So, as Luther asks so frequently in the Small Catechism, what does this mean?

Surprisingly, you won't necessarily find the word "concordia" in the Bible, at least not in English. But would it surprise you, nonetheless, if I said that it is indeed biblical? I served for nine years as a missionary of the LCMS in the Dominican Republic, preaching and teaching in the Spanish language. One quick search of the Spanish RVR1960 Bible (that's kind of like the Spanish equivalent of our King James Bible!) turned up a reference to "concordia" in 2 Corinthians 6:15. There, St. Paul is asking, "What *accord* has Christ with Belial" (ESV). "Belial" is another name for Satan, a Hebrew word that means wicked or worthless. What *concordia* has Christ with Satan? The NIV uses the word "agreement," and the NRSV uses the word "harmony." The Greek word behind all those terms is literally the basis of our English word "symphony." Interestingly, the Romans believed in a goddess named Concordia who embodied agreement in marriage and society. The corresponding Greek goddess was called Harmony. But it is the one true God who is the source of all concordia, the principal player who makes beautiful music in all that He does.

Earlier, I mentioned that concordia is a word of importance from the Reformation onward. However, understanding the term as "harmony" takes us much further back, back to the beginning. In the beginning was concordia. No, the actual term 'concordia' is not found in the text of Genesis. But everything that God created clearly enjoyed concordia. God created the heavens and the earth, as well as plants, animals, including fish, birds, and various creepy-crawly creatures. Finally, He created human beings, male and female. He created them in His own image, to be reflections of Himself in their life together in the beautiful creation. Everything was building up to this.

God placed the crown of His creation in the lush Garden of Eden, a place of abundant blessing, a place where He dwelt in their midst. "Eden" literally means luxury, delicacy, and delight. God gave them everything they needed for their good. That's what it means to have a God, to receive all good from Him. He also gave them dominion over the creation—animals and even the land. On the sixth day, God looked at everything that He had made, and it was "very good" (Genesis 1:31). There was concordia between God, humanity, and all creation. Imagine a beautiful symphony where all the musical parts are in harmony. Everything fits together and works together to produce a joyous end—a delightful sound that is pleasing to the ear. Symphony! Harmony! Concordia!

Now imagine Beethoven's Fifth Symphony cutting off suddenly after those first two intense introductory measures instead of launching into the ingenious development of that dramatic, well-known, twice-repeated opening theme: da da da dah…da da da dah. God placed two special trees in the midst of the Garden: the Tree of Life and the Tree of the Knowledge of Good and Evil (Genesis 2:9). He commanded the man and the woman not to eat of the Tree of the Knowledge of Good and Evil, for eating from it meant death. But what God did is not what stopped the music. Concordia means trusting God, taking Him at His Word. It wasn't blind obedience. Rather, it was a firm faith. God's voice and humanity's were in concert. The man and woman sang the same song, echoing back to God all He had voiced to them. But then another voice thundered in unexpectedly. It was the discordant voice of the serpent: "Did God really say?" Stop the music! Unfortunately, that's what happened. The man and the woman heeded the strange voice. They preferred a different tune. They ate of the fruit of the Tree of the Knowledge of Good and Evil. Concordia was no more.

It was a tragedy of cosmic proportions. The man and woman traded concordia for discord. They traded God's way for their own way. They traded faith for unbelief. Was God holding something back? Faith says no. Faith doesn't even ask that question. Faith humbly receives what God gives, thanks and praises Him for it. Faith abounds in love for God and neighbor. Faith rejoices in concordia! Faith sings God's song, loudly and proudly. Tragically, the music literally stopped, and everything fell out of sync. God's voice soon rang out once again, but the man and woman closed their ears and hid in fear. "In the day that you eat of it you shall surely die" (Genesis 2:17). They no longer rejoiced in the goodness of God. Instead, they anticipated wrath. The serpent is cursed. The ground is cursed. The whole creation falls under the curse of death. The man and woman are expelled from the Garden, barred from the presence of God, and no longer in earshot of His voice. Instead, countless discordant voices take the stage.

Thankfully, God uttered one more sweet sound. It was directed to the serpent. The serpent, no doubt, hated this new theme. But it was a delightful melody for all creation, especially humanity, a melody that will be developed through the rest of the story of God's people: "I will put enmity between you and the woman, and between your offspring and her offspring; he shall bruise your head, and you shall bruise his heel" (Genesis 3:15). It was the key to a new song, concordia restored. The woman's offspring will sing a new song. He will triumph over all other discordant music. His song will stay at the top of the charts for all eternity. It's the song the whole creation will sing for all eternity (see Psalm 148).

Poetic prophets inspired by God will embellish the song, revealing more and more of its melody and lyrics in the centuries to come. But other voices still ring out. So God chooses a man named Abram, yanks him out of all the idolatrous noise, and promises to make him a great singer, with a chorus of descendants, and a venue to be heard. His descendants will sing the sweet new song on the world stage. Sadly, Israel couldn't stay in sync. Those other voices and melodies got the better of many of them. Israel wanted to sing the songs of their neighbors. They preferred concordia with wicked nations, who long ago closed their ears to God's new song and drowned it out with their favorite tunes.

But there's a plot twist. Just when it seems that God's enchanting new song is silenced, God reintroduces His melody in a still, small way, but with incredibly powerful effect. Come to find out, a few faithful Israelites who long for concordia are still singing His song. An angel tells a young virgin that she will be with child, and she breaks out in song: "My soul magnifies the Lord, and my spirit rejoices in God my Savior...He has helped His servant Israel in remembrance of His mercy, as He spoke to our fathers, to Abraham and to his offspring forever" (Luke 1:46–55). Concordia! God sends another voice, a prelude to sing a song of preparation: "In the wilderness prepare the way of the Lord" (Isaiah 40:3). Concordia! John the Baptist's father, Zechariah, sang too: "Blessed be the Lord God of Israel, for He has visited and redeemed His people and has raised up a horn of salvation for us in the house of his servant David" (Luke 1:68–69). Concordia!

Jesus sang hymns with His disciples. He sang God's song. In fact, He was God's song incarnate. "In him was life, and the life was the light of men. The light shines in the darkness, and the darkness has not overcome it" (John 1:45). That means that no other song could drown Him out. But some of His own people still closed their ears. The serpent went one more round to silence God's song. But Jesus was the fulfillment, the culmination of that sweet song God sang in Genesis 3:15, announcing the serpent's fate. Jesus sang God's song all the way to the cross. No, he didn't open His mouth, just as Isaiah prophesied (Isaiah 53:7). He uttered a few words from the cross, but ultimately He sang God's song by believing, trusting God, doing His heavenly Father's will of paying for the sins of the world, dying our death, and crushing the serpent's head. He sang God's song all the way to the cross where He cried out, "It is finished" (John 19:30). But death didn't silence the song. Jesus truly died, but He didn't stay dead. God raised Him to life again, and His song of victory can never be silenced.

Now the song of the gospel rings out with a crescendo to all corners of the earth. We here on earth, thousands of years later, can still hear its sweet sound. Holy Baptism has brought us into the chorus. Sure, other songs are still playing, but they cannot overcome Him. Jesus, who ascended to the right hand of God, still comes down among us. The whole company of heaven breaks into the ranks of God's army, you and me, still fighting the good fight of faith here below. God's song sounds forth when your pastor speaks (or even sings!) Jesus' words: "This is my body, given for you. This is the new testament in my blood, shed for you for the forgiveness of sins." And you and I sing: "O Christ, the Lamb of God, who takes away the sins of the world, have mercy." We receive Him and sing "Amen, it shall be so."

Sometimes, like Israel of old, we're tempted, lured in by the songs of our unbelieving neighbors. That's what happens when you sin against God and neighbor: when you lie to your parents, when you covet your friend's new car, when you lust after someone who isn't your spouse, and the list goes on. That's a different song. That's the chorus of death and defeat, not victory and life. Repent! Rejoice that God, in Christ, has redeemed you from sin and death. He has forgiven your sins. He has made you part of the heavenly chorus—no need to audition. You are chosen. You are in the choir. His Spirit keeps you in the faith, trusting Him, believing Him, clinging to Him for all that is good, and singing His praises forever. Concordia!

Jesus is your concordia with God! He even prays that you'll be as in harmony with Him and with your fellow believers as He is with the Father (John 17:20–21). In Jesus, you are never tone deaf. You are never out of sync. He fills you with good things, and you overflow with songs of praise. King David sang that God "put a new song in my mouth, a song of praise to our God. Many will see and fear, and put their trust in the Lord" (Psalm 40:3). God's song indeed goes out and never returns empty. So, sing, dear saint. Let your concordia ring out to the ends of the earth!

Sing with all the saints in glory,
Sing the resurrection song!
(LSB 671:1)

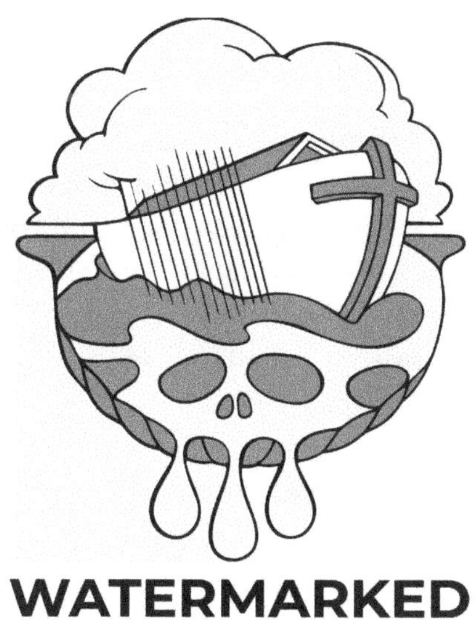

The Both/And Reality of Faith

Rev. Harrison Goodman

Mostly, we talk about the end of Matthew as ‘the great commission.” Go baptize and teach all nations. Make the kingdom bigger. It's easy to get caught up in the excitement of the moment and forget who Jesus is talking to. The baptismal formula is introduced to doubters who came out to worship the risen Lord.

Matthew 28:17–20: “And when they saw him they worshiped him, but some doubted. And Jesus came and said to them, “All authority in heaven and on earth has been given to me. Go therefore and make disciples of all nations, baptizing them in the name of the Father and of the Son and of the Holy Spirit, teaching them to observe all that I have commanded you. And behold, I am with you always, to the end of the age.”

They worshipped Him. But some doubted. It wasn't that one thing happened, then the other. Simultaneously, there was worship and doubt. Simultaneously, they were sinner and saint. It's important to set expectations. This is what the Christian life is like. Christ would ascend into heaven, and the 12 wouldn't see Him again until the Last Day. They showed up to church anxious, doubting, and sinning. That wouldn't stop this side of glory. They would be both sinners and saints every day until they fell asleep. And since being left alone with that particular both/and is soul-crushing, Jesus leaves His disciples the Gift of Baptism as He ascends to sit at the right hand of the Father. He makes them a promise. In Baptism, He will be with them always, even unto the end of the age.

Baptism isn't the pledge we make to be good Christians. It isn't a fresh start and a second chance to do better this time. Baptism is for the lives of Christians that don't line up so nicely with all our best-laid plans to be better. Baptism is a washing for your mess. It's for the chaos of feeling warring loves as you stare down the sin you can't shake. Baptism is for the loneliness of quietly glancing down the pew and wondering why nobody else seems to doubt like you doubt, worry like you worry, sin like you sin. Baptism is for the abject terror of being found out for the things you really think, really feel, really do. Baptism is for you as you live your "both/and" "sinner/saint" life. It's all a mess. We show up to worship, full of anxiety, guilt, and shame, the same as the 12. We show up frauds and hypocrites. And we show up saints because we show up baptized. Baptism is a life-giving water, rich in grace, and a washing of the new birth in the Holy Spirit. It is how God saves you. Forgives you. And He does it daily, which allows us to talk about who He gives it to—the ones who need forgiveness every day. We are watermarked. Every day. It's an identity that's chaos in you and blessedly simple in the font.

Identity in the Font

That's why God would not have you build your identity based on how Christian you feel or even how Christian you act. Insecurities live where the law rules. If it's up to me to prove my faith by my works, every sin is tangible doubt. If it's up to me to feel committed to God, every other ungodly love I have to hide out of shame of being found out is proof of just how unchristian I am. If God's love is tied to how Christian you feel and act, whenever you need God the most, He will always feel the farthest away.

So He ties your identity to His actions, not yours. His heart, not yours. He ties your salvation to water and word. Baptism now saves you. Because Jesus says so. You are simultaneously sinner and saint. You believe. And you doubt. You strive to love God and neighbor. And you sin. But it's not about you. It's about Jesus for you. The disciples showed up to worship while also doubting. And they were only called the disciples. Their identity wasn't measured in whether or not they felt or acted Christian. It was in the fact that Jesus called them disciples. So they were.

Baptism is where He calls you His child, and so you are. It's where He delivers the salvation He won for you on the cross. Both are necessary. Not just a cross. A cross for you. It matters that Jesus took on human flesh and human sin to die for you and for all upon a cross, winning your forgiveness. But the cross can feel far away. You weren't there. Even the disciples that were largely fled. So Jesus delivers that forgiveness through water and word to you and all. Both are necessary. Salvation won that you can't lay hold of is all but worthless to you. So God gives you Baptism to deliver salvation through time and space so you can actually lay hold of it and rest in it when everything else is a mess and your hands and your heart are clearly not enough. You're enough anyway. Because Jesus calls you enough. Baptized. Forgiven, so there is no more sin. Holy, so there is nothing left that's unclean. Saint, so you're already brought through death and all its trappings. Because you are baptized. God's work to join His word to water to give you something more than you can build or be on your own. He adopts you as His child here. That becomes the only thing left to define you. Your identity is baptized. Your identity is in Christ. Because to be in Baptism is to be in Christ.

Galatians 3:27: "For as many of you as were baptized into Christ have put on Christ."

You put on Christ. You wear Him. You are baptized. Jesus says, "Here, I am with you. Here, I am your identity. Your peace. Your hope. Your holiness. Your life." Whether or not you feel it, He is not far, but near. He is not measured in your hands or your heart but in the water and the word. Baptism is not just plain water, but it is the water included in God's command and combined with God's word. God joins His word to water to make sure that wherever there is water, there can also be hope. Measure God's presence not in your success or your heart, but in His promise. He is in the font. You who are baptized wear Christ. You might feel and act like a sinner, but God insists you are only called saint.

When you daily struggle with sin. When it's the websites you can't stay away from. The attractions you can't ignore. The hatred that shouldn't live in your heart but hides behind everything that reminds you of what hurt you. When you can only see the places you keep failing. You are baptized. God is daily forgiving you, making you new, clean, and holy, all here. Baptism isn't just a symbol. It doesn't remind you of God's forgiveness. It gives it. Baptism becomes the mark of your identity as a Christian. Forgiven. Righteous. Your identity is saint.

It's not just for what you've done. It's for what's been done to you, too. It's the answer to one of the great mistakes we make around victims. The first thing we tell the ones who have experienced atrocities like molestation and rape is that it's not their fault. And that is completely true. And completely unhelpful. Because they still feel unclean. It might not be their fault, but it is their burden. An identity sullied by something from the outside in. So God washes and makes new and clean and holy from the outside in, too. Every day. Your identity is not "less" or "unclean". You are baptized. Your identity is in the font. Your identity is in Christ.

Make the sign of the cross and remember your Baptism. That's all the sign is. A reminder. You are baptized. Nothing can change that now. Nothing can take away from that. Nothing needs to add to it. Water has marked you. This is who you are.

Already dead. Not dead yet.

You are dead to sin. You are alive to God in Christ. Not symbolically. Literally.

Romans 6:3–5: "Do you not know that all of us who have been baptized into Christ Jesus were baptized into his death? We were buried therefore with him by Baptism into death, in order that, just as Christ was raised from the dead by the glory of the Father, we too might walk in newness of life. For if we have been united with him in a death like his, we shall certainly be united with him in a resurrection like his."

Baptism isn't a symbol of Christ's death being your death. You *were buried* with Him. In your Baptism, you already died. If you've ever seen a Baptism, you've seen a death. It was just unremarkable because Christ broke death. Death doesn't work anymore. Christ is risen. Because you're baptized, you rise too. Baptism makes Christ's death your death. Baptism makes Christ's resurrection your resurrection. So death is defeated for you. Death is an unremarkable enemy now. And all those things today that make you feel so far from Christ, so alone, and so unclean? In Baptism, those become unremarkable, too. The pains and evils and anxieties and hurts and even the sins you keep committing. You are already through them. Ask yourself, "Can they keep Jesus in the tomb? Can they undo His death and resurrection?" Because you're tied to His victory. So if all those things that are way too big for you can't keep Jesus in the tomb, they can't stop you from rising either. They can't take this Gift from you. So this Gift must be to face them. Your Baptism isn't fragile. It can stand against all these things. They can't break it. You're baptized. You're already through them. All the way to the tomb and back out again. Dead to sin. Alive to God in Christ Jesus.

Baptism is a "both/and" reality for "both/and" Christians. You sinner/saints are already dead and already alive again. Baptism indicates that the Old Adam in us should by daily contrition and repentance be drowned and die with all sins and evil desires, and that a new man should daily emerge and arise to live before God in righteousness and purity forever. Note the word daily. The Christian doesn't just die once. He dies daily. Which means Old Adam, who drowns, is a strong swimmer. We always want to measure the places Old Adam needs to drown again because he swam back up. That's the thing that makes it so dangerous to measure in you instead of measure in the font. We always need to hear the promise that Baptism drowns him daily, and raises you up holy every day, too. Old Adam can't stay dead yet. Not until you fall asleep or the last great day. But you can't stay dead ever. Just as unremarkable as the first death was, so will be the second. Because Jesus has made it so. The worst is already over. What remains is as trivial as a nap until the resurrection. It's important to set expectations. Baptized, you will rise. The life of the Christian will be full of sin and sorrow. The victory is still secure. Measure it in the font, not in you. God has joined His promise to water. As long as water is wet, you can hope.

Beyond the Balancing Scales

Rev. Matt Richard

Balancing the Scales?

We sure make a mess of things when somebody sins against us. That is to say, instead of looking toward forgiveness, we typically go the way of revenge.

Here is how it works with us. Somebody sins against us. What the specific sin and circumstances are do not matter at this point. What matters is that somebody has wronged us. And so, what happens after we have been sinned against is that we immediately magnify their offense. We make their sin big—no, we make their sin very big—while at the same time downplaying our sins. We become self-righteous in thinking that we would never do to others what has just been done to us, and we make sure to let everyone else know this, too.

After we have been wronged, we hold on to the other person's sin. We keep it tightly clenched in our fists so that we can analyze their sin and the circumstances surrounding it to determine a fair price for it. In other words, they sinned against us, which means that they now owe us a payment to make up for what they have done.

The exact amount of the payment or the way that they can pay for their sins is usually determined in our mind after we have had time to mull it over. If we think it is a big sin, then their payment will be significant. If small, we may consider taking a lower payment or waiving the fee altogether. The point is that they have offended us and must do or say something to pay it off so that we can let go of the offense in our minds.

And if they don't pay? Well, we laugh in our minds with glee because that means that we now have the right to get revenge on them for their sins. They sinned against us, and they won't pay the payment, so now we are free to enact a penalty on them. After all, they have it coming!

In our minds, the scales must always be balanced. By sinning against us, the other person has unbalanced the scales of justice. To balance the scales, they must give something back to us, or we must take something from them to make things right again. Thus, we become fixated on keeping track of everyone who sins against us. In our mind, we catalog all the people who sin against us, along with the payment they owe us to be made right again.

If a person makes their payment, they may earn back our good graces. If they don't make their payment, well... we will be gracious by not seeking revenge right away, but by giving them the cold shoulder, or perhaps talking behind their back to send them a message to pay up. And if they don't pick up on our cold shoulder and our passive-aggressive behavior, we may then make a plan to penalize them for not paying up. The plan may hurt them and their reputation, but we have no other choice but to punish them because justice must be served. Somebody must uphold righteousness, somebody must stand up to them, and it must be us!

The Danger of Unforgiveness

But here is where we must pause and ask a critical question: What happens to us when we live in this cycle of debt and revenge? Over time, the heart begins to harden. The soul becomes entangled in self-righteousness, as if we are the ultimate judge and jury over our neighbor's sins. It produces a grim religion of works—a theology where others must earn our grace, and where we deny them mercy unless they reach a bar that we ourselves could never meet. In doing so, we set ourselves in the place of God.

This is the subtle and dangerous deception of unforgiveness. It parades as justice, but at its root is pride and a denial of the Gospel. The longer we carry someone else's offense as our own burden, the more it festers and shapes our identities around being victims. We stop seeing ourselves as sinners who have been rescued and start seeing ourselves as moral gatekeepers to whom the world owes restitution.

Now, it is clear that living a life of revenge is not only sinful but toxic. Living a life of revenge demands that you are always on the lookout for those who sin against you. Instead of love covering a multitude of sins, vengeance seeks out every possible offense against you. Instead of putting the best construction on situations and other people, this life of vengeance seeks out every possible way to get dirt on others and be offended. When this happens, grace has no place in you, and you end up giving yourself into bitterness and a toxic self-righteousness that leads straight to Hell.

A Parable

This is why we pray in the Fifth Petition of the Lord's Prayer that the Lord would forgive us our trespasses as we forgive those who trespass against us. And this is precisely what a parable in the Gospel of Matthew teaches us.

> Then Peter came up and said to him, "Lord, how often will my brother sin against me, and I forgive him? As many as seven times?" Jesus said to him, "I do not say to you seven times, but seventy-seven times. "Therefore, the kingdom of heaven may be compared to a king who wished to settle accounts with his servants. When he began to settle, one was brought to him who owed him ten thousand talents. And since he could not pay, his master ordered him to be sold, with his

> wife and children and all that he had, and payment to be made. So the servant fell on his knees, imploring him, 'Have patience with me, and I will pay you everything.' And out of pity for him, the master of that servant released him and forgave him the debt. But when that same servant went out, he found one of his fellow servants who owed him a hundred denarii, and seizing him, he began to choke him, saying, 'Pay what you owe.' So his fellow servant fell down and pleaded with him, 'Have patience with me, and I will pay you.' He refused and went and put him in prison until he should pay the debt. When his fellow servants saw what had taken place, they were greatly distressed, and they went and reported to their master all that had taken place. Then his master summoned him and said to him, 'You wicked servant! I forgave you all that debt because you pleaded with me. And should not you have had mercy on your fellow servant, as I had mercy on you?' And in anger his master delivered him to the jailers, until he should pay all his debt. So also my heavenly Father will do to every one of you, if you do not forgive your brother from your heart." (Matthew 18:21-35)

In the Gospel of Matthew, we hear of a servant who was forgiven a debt of what is equivalent to over seven billion dollars in today's money. Yet, this very same servant would not forgive another fellow servant of a mere twelve thousand dollars in debt. In other words, the servant was forgiven an astronomical amount by his master, but was unwilling to forgive another servant for a minimal debt.

This is why the master called out the servant as being wicked. He was not only called out for having a wicked heart but was also called out for being actively evil, hurtful, diseased, and ethically blind. There was a tremendous inconsistency with his heart. He gladly received from the gracious master and ruthlessly took from his fellow slave—pure wickedness!

Frankly stated, when we go the way of revenge, vengeance, and unforgiveness, we are not only acting like the unforgiving servant but are exemplifying the same wicked heart. Keeping a record of everyone's sins in one hand while receiving the Body and Blood of Christ in the other hand is not only inconsistent but reveals the evil of our sinful natures. There is a profound contradiction in holding on to grudges in one hand and holding on to forgiveness in the other.

So, what must we do? The answer is that we must forgive one another.

However, an important note is needed. Indeed, significant harm has been done to Christians when forgiveness is confused with things that it is not.

What Forgiveness is Not

For example, forgiveness is not the same as friendship. When you forgive a person, you are letting go of revenge and the need for them to pay off their sin to you. You are releasing your desire to get even with them through penalties. In other words, this forgiveness may or may not lead to a great friendship. If you become great friends through forgiveness, God be praised. If not, God be praised that you have forgiven one another and are forgiven in Christ.

Forgiveness is also not forgetting. When God forgives, He forgets; however, when we forgive, we are letting go of revenge. This means that there will be times when forgiveness leads to forgetfulness and other times when it does not and should not. For instance, a person—by God's grace—can forgive someone who abused them, but probably should not let that person babysit their children. You can forgive and still have wise boundaries against the tendency or patterns of other people's old Adam.

Forgiveness also does not mean that a person should be automatically free from the consequences of their actions. You can forgive someone, and they may still face charges under civil law. Forgiveness does not erase legal accountability.

And finally, forgiveness is not brushing something under the carpet as if it never happened. Forgiveness is the exact opposite. You only forgive where there is sin. If there is no sin, no forgiveness is required.

Christ Balances the Scales, Which Means Freedom - For You

Think about forgiveness in the following manner: Your sins have made justice unbalanced. Your sins demand payment before God.

And God, in His wrath, would be completely justified to smite you. But Christ, who is rich in mercy and abounding in love, balanced the scales, made a payment, and satisfied wrath for you—completely—through His death and resurrection, which results in your forgiveness.

And forgiveness? It is God letting go of vengeance toward you. Forgiveness is God erasing your debt. Forgiveness is God releasing you from penalty. Forgiveness is God loosening the demand. Forgiveness is equal to the simple word: "Freedom!"

And this is what you have in Christ: freedom. Christ has freed you from the vengeance of God, the debt of your sin, and the demands of the Law. In Christ, this is what you get to deliver to others who have sinned against you—forgiveness. Freedom.

The man in the parable was forgiven seven billion dollars in debt, which showed that there was no limit to his forgiveness of other people's small debts. Indeed, there is more forgiveness of sins in Jesus than you and your neighbor have sins. There is no sin that you and your neighbor have committed that is so deep that it escapes the blood of Mount Calvary. The blood of Mount Calvary is the payment that atones for every single one of your sins—and your neighbor's—in thought, word, and deed, from the past, present, and future.

And so, you have been forgiven all of your sins in Christ Jesus so that you can forgive one another—not out of compulsion but out of the love and forgiveness given to you first.

Only forgiven people can forgive.

Only loved people can love.

You forgive because there is more grace in Christ than there are sins in you and in your neighbor.

Forgiveness for you; forgiveness for your neighbor; all because of Christ.

For You 2022

Rev. Todd Peperkorn

When someone says something is FOR YOU, what do they mean? It might be a birthday present, a paycheck, or even a bill or an invitation. If something is FOR YOU, that means it is somehow personal, that it is directed and specific, it isn't just for EVERYONE. It means something that has been given to you.

In some ways, we live in a FOR YOU world. It's called the algorithm. Every time you open TikTok, Instagram, Snapchat, or Facebook, the algorithm is figuring out what exactly to show you so that you will stay on the platform.

This FOR YOU may be targeted, but it is not for your good. You could even argue that it is against you, not for you.

That is not what Jesus means when He died and rose again from the dead FOR YOU. Let's hear from God's Word what He has to say about it.

FOR YOU in the Bible

It doesn't matter really if something is there unless it is there FOR YOU. This expression has always held a special place in God's Word, and really for Lutherans. Already at the Exodus and the Passover, God said,

> The blood shall be a sign for you, on the houses where you are. And when I see the blood, I will pass over you, and no plague will befall you to destroy you, when I strike the land of Egypt. (Exodus 12:13)

The blood marked the people of Israel so that they would not die from the tenth plague. The blood literally kept them alive. It did not matter if there was blood on the doorposts of the house next door. It needed to be their house. They needed to be marked. It needed to be for them.

Jesus' death and resurrection are FOR YOU. God's promises are not generic. We hear in John 3:16 that God loved the world in that He gave His only-begotten Son over to death. But in the same way, we hear St. Paul express it like this in Galatians:

> I have been crucified with Christ. It is no longer I who live, but Christ who lives in me. And the life I now live in the flesh I live by faith in the Son of God, who loved me and gave himself for me. (Galatians 2:20)

There is an individuality to this message of hope. If I can understand that God is for me, then I can understand the nature of how God works in the world through the church.

FOR YOU in the Creed and Luther

But it is more we than me. God's love is for the world, and it is FOR YOU. Because God loves you, He gives Himself over to death and the grave for you. We put it this way in the Nicene Creed:

"…who for us men and for our salvation came down from heaven and was incarnate by the Holy Spirit of the Virgin Mary and was made man…"

In other words, Jesus came down from heaven FOR YOU. Martin Luther put it this way in his great Easter hymn, "Christ Jesus Lay in Death's Strong Bands":

Here our true Paschal Lamb we see,
Whom God so freely gave us;
He died on the accursèd tree—
So strong His love—to save us.
See, His blood now marks our door;
Faith points to it; death passes o'er,
And Satan cannot harm us.
Alleluia!

Luther also put it this way in the Small Catechism: "He has redeemed me, a lost and condemned creature, purchased and won me from all sins, from death, and from the power of the devil."

Notice how these two things weave back and forth, me and we. It is for you personally, but you are not alone. You are now grafted into the Body of Christ, into His church. There is no FOR YOU really unless it is also FOR Y'ALL. I know that isn't really a word, but you get the point.

FOR YOU in Baptism and the Sacrament

It is still easy to think of this as abstract, as an idea that doesn't have flesh and blood. God, therefore, applies this salvation to you in Holy Baptism.

Think of what happens in Holy Baptism. The pastor puts the sign of the cross on you and marks you as one redeemed by Christ, the crucified. He calls you out by name when you are baptized. There is no question who it is for. It is FOR YOU, along with all of the promises that God gives in Holy Baptism.

But there is still more! In the Lord's Supper, we have it right there in the Words of Institution:

> Our Lord Jesus Christ, on the night He was betrayed, took bread, and when He had given thanks, He broke it and gave it to the disciples and said: "Take, eat; this is my body, which is given for you. This do in remembrance of me."

> In the same way also, He took the cup after supper, and when He had given thanks, He gave it to them, saying: "Drink of it, all of you; this is My blood of the New Testament, which is shed for you for the forgiveness of sins. This do, as often as you drink it, in remembrance of Me." (Matthew 26:26-28; Mark 14:22-24; Luke 22:19-20; 1 Corinthians 11:23-25)

It is a little hard to understand in English, but that for you in the Words of Institution could really be translated "for y'all." He gives His body to the church, and in doing this, the church becomes His body.

This is why there is such a close relationship with you, the church, and your neighbor. In one sermon, Luther talks about this like understanding the making of bread. This is an image that St. Paul uses as well when he writes:

> "The cup of blessing that we bless, is it not a participation in the blood of Christ? The bread that we break, is it not a participation in the body of Christ?" (1 Corinthians 10:16)

When we break the bread (that is, eat it), we now participate in the body of Christ. That word translated participate is the word koinonia in Greek. It is usually translated as either fellowship or even communion. We are now the body of Christ. Luther writes about it this way:

> "The Holy Sacrament produces two things: one is that it makes us brothers and fellow heirs of the Lord Christ, such that it makes us one cake with him; the other that we also become common and one with all other people upon earth and also all become one cake." (Luther, 1523 sermon)

He then goes on:

> "You know that when a person bakes bread all the grain is thoroughly ground. Thus each kernel becomes flour with all the others, and thus all are mixed together so that in one sack full of flour the grain is so mixed and thrown together that each becomes the flour of the other.

> No kernel retains its form. Each gives to the other its flour and each loses its own body...I give myself for the common good and serve you and you make use of what is mine of which you are in need."

I really like this image, because it means that I am always a part of something bigger than myself. God takes me, grinds me up, and then makes me a part of His very Body and Blood. So, when I go to Communion, I leave my sins and hardships, and I pick up my neighbor's sins and hardships. Isn't that amazing?

FOR YOU Means Trust

One of the things that is hard about it, though, is that this also has to do with trust. God calls me to trust that He is going to take care of me through my neighbor. St. Paul writes about this in Philippians:

> "...do not be anxious about anything, but in everything by prayer and supplication with thanksgiving let your requests be made known to God." (Philippians 4:6)

In other words, when anxiety creeps in, when worry and doubt start to rear their ugly head, God invites us to tell Him about it. Our instinct is to retreat, to hide, to curl up into our own shell so that we can feel safe, at least for a teeny, little while.

What our heavenly Father knows, though, is that curling up in a little ball may feel good for a brief moment, but it won't satisfy. It won't make you safe. It won't turn problems away. It won't bring you hope. Only He can do that. And He invites you to come into His house and receive His Body and Blood, for by doing that, you are drawn up into Him, and we are drawn into each other.

This is why the message of FOR YOU matters so much today. In many respects, it seems like we lost the point of FOR YOU during COVID. Even though it was five years ago (as of this writing), it still shapes us and how we think about the world.

For many, the COVID-19 time was a time when we learned to stay home. We learned to be alone. We may have even learned that the other people don't help; they actually make things worse!

And so, we can convince ourselves that by being alone, I am going to be safe.

But that is the lie, and that is why understanding the FOR YOU of the Gospel is so important today. All the way back in the Garden, God said, ". . . It is not good that the man should be alone; I will make him a helper fit for him."(Genesis 2:18) This isn't about men and women right now so much as it is about how we are made. We are made as human beings to be in communion with Him and with each other.

For You, For Each Other

God invites you to see that His plan is for you. He knows what you need better than you even know yourself. He knows your fears and anxieties. He knows your doubts and despair. He knows it all, and more.

Because He knows, He gives Himself for you, so that you may be freed to receive His Gifts and love your neighbor. It is impossible to serve those around you if you are constantly afraid and despairing of your own place in this wide world of ours. He then takes this up, makes you a part of Himself, and in doing this, brings you into fellowship with the whole Christian church in this whole wide world.

It's a pretty crazy idea, isn't it? But that is the nature of the gospel. In the Gospels of Jesus Christ, there is always more to come, because God's love for you knows no bounds, has no limits or barriers that can hold it, that is, Him, back.

Perhaps the final stanza of hymn 544 from our hymnal can express it best for us:

> All glory to our Lord and God
> For love so deep, so high, so broad;
> The Trinity whom we adore
> Forever and forevermore. (LSB 544:7)

The Existence of God and Deity of Jesus

Dr. Adam Francisco

I. Why This Matters

Skepticism is all around us. In classrooms, on social media, and in popular culture, the idea that belief in God and, more specifically, in the Christian claim that God became man in Jesus Christ is reasonable is often dismissed outright. For many students, the very thought of affirming such beliefs feels intellectually risky, perhaps even naïve. "Science has explained or someday will explain everything," some say. "Religion is just a human invention," others add. And occasionally, the objection comes in a more personal form: "I can't see God, so how can I believe?"

These are real questions that deserve serious answers. Christianity has never asked its followers to shut off their brains or to embrace blind faith. On the contrary, the Christian claim has always been that God created a world of order, beauty, and meaning, and that He has revealed Himself in such a way that belief is not only possible but compelling. Far from being irrational, the conviction that God exists and that He has come among us in the person of Jesus Christ stands on ground that is, apologetically speaking, beyond reasonable doubt.

In what follows, we will examine the evidence in three movements. First, we will consider why belief in God is reasonable and even necessary given what we know about the universe and human existence. Second, we will turn to the historical evidence for Jesus, showing that the Christian claim about His incarnation is not legend but reality. Finally, we will see how these truths converge to make sense of life itself.

II. The Case for God's Existence

The Cosmos

One of the most basic questions at the intersection of science and religion is, "Why is there something rather than nothing?" Everything in our experience has an explanation, and when we look at the universe itself, the same logic applies. Scientific discoveries in the last century have only reinforced this. The universe is not eternal. It had a beginning, a point at which time, space, and matter came into existence. The widely accepted theory of the Big Bang points to a moment of origin. The second law of thermodynamics likewise suggests the universe is running down—like a clock that was wound up but is slowly unwinding.

What wound it up? What stands behind the universe? The cause must be outside time, space, and matter since these themselves began. It must be powerful enough to bring the universe into existence and personal enough to choose to create. The best explanation is God. To deny this requires believing that the universe simply appeared uncaused, which is far less reasonable than acknowledging a transcendent Creator.

Design

The more we learn about the universe, the more finely tuned it appears. The constants of physics—gravity, electromagnetism, the ratio of matter to antimatter—are tuned so precisely that even the smallest alteration would render life impossible. Imagine a dial board with dozens of knobs. Each knob must be set at exactly the right level, or the whole system fails. The odds of this happening by accident are astronomically small.

Or think of the universe like a grand symphony. Every instrument must be perfectly tuned and play its part at just the right moment for the music to exist. If even one violin is off-key or a trumpet comes in at the wrong time, the harmony collapses. In the same way, the constants of the universe must all be exactly right. The fact that they are is no accident—it is the mark of a Composer.

Life itself tells the same story. At the heart of every cell is DNA, an information code more complex than the most advanced computer program. We know from experience that codes come from minds, not from blind chance. The design of the universe points to a Designer.

Morality

Beyond physics and biology, there is the human conscience. Across cultures and centuries, people have recognized certain actions as right and others as wrong. Of course, societies differ on details, but the core moral truths—honesty, justice, and the wrongness of murder—are universal. If morality were nothing more than a product of evolution, we might expect some communities to celebrate dishonesty or cruelty as virtues. Yet we don't.

Why? Because morality is not invented; it is discovered. It reflects a standard beyond ourselves. If objective moral values exist, they require a moral lawgiver whose character grounds them. Once again, the best explanation is God.

Taken together, these arguments from cosmology, design, and morality provide cumulative evidence. They do not merely make God plausible; they make His existence the most reasonable conclusion.

III. God Was in Christ Jesus

Admitting that some kind of god exists is one thing. Why, one could honestly ask, does it have to be the Christian God? Couldn't the Designer be Allah, or some impersonal force, or simply "the universe" itself?

The Christian claim is unique. It is not just that God exists but that He has revealed Himself decisively in history. Christianity is not a set of abstract ideas or moral rules; it is the proclamation that God became man in Jesus of Nazareth. No other religion makes such a claim. Philosophers offer arguments about truth. Prophets deliver moral teaching. But Christians say: God Himself entered human history, took on flesh, walked among us, died for us, and rose from the dead.

This claim is bold. If false, Christianity collapses. But if true, it means the Creator of the cosmos has made Himself known. And unlike vague notions of spirituality, the incarnation can be tested historically. If God became man, there should be evidence. And there is.

Sources and Early Witnesses

First, we must ask: Do we have reliable records about Jesus? The answer is yes. The New Testament documents, particularly the Gospels and Paul's letters, were written within a generation of Jesus' life. Scholars generally agree that Paul's letters, some of which date to the 50s AD, preserve traditions from even earlier. In fact, the creed recorded in 1 Corinthians 15, which summarizes Jesus' death, burial, and resurrection appearances, likely originated within five years of the crucifixion.

Outside the New Testament, non-Christian historians confirm Jesus' existence. The Roman historian Tacitus records that Christ was executed under Pontius Pilate. The Jewish historian Josephus likewise mentions Jesus and His followers. Pliny the Younger, writing to the emperor Trajan, notes that early Christians worshiped Christ "as a god." These are not friendly witnesses, yet they corroborate the core facts.

The Reality of the Incarnation

What did Jesus Himself claim? He was not content to be regarded as a teacher of morals. He forgave sins—something only God could do. He identified Himself with God by using divine titles. He accepted worship. When His opponents accused Him of blasphemy, they understood His claims exactly.

C.S. Lewis once pointed out that a man who said the things Jesus said could not be merely a great moral teacher. He must be either a liar, a lunatic, or the Lord. The historical record shows no evidence of delusion or deceit. What remains is that He is who He said He was: God in flesh.

"But in Fact, Christ Has Been Raised"

The decisive evidence for Jesus' divine identity is the resurrection. After His crucifixion, His followers were devastated and afraid. Yet within weeks, they were boldly proclaiming that He was alive. What explains this transformation?

For starters, the empty tomb. Even the opponents of Christianity acknowledged it, claiming the disciples had stolen the body—a concession that the tomb was in fact empty. The appearances of Jesus to individuals and groups, including skeptics like James and persecutors like Paul, are well attested. Most compelling is the explosive growth of the early church, which willingly suffered persecution and death for their conviction that they had encountered the risen Christ.

Alternative explanations collapse under scrutiny. Hallucinations do not happen in groups. Conspiracies unravel under pressure, yet none of the disciples recanted. Legends take centuries to develop, yet the resurrection was proclaimed from the very beginning. The resurrection is the best explanation of the evidence, and it confirms Jesus' claim to be God incarnate.

IV. The Coherence of the Christian Worldview

Philosophically, the incarnation resolves tensions that no other worldview can. How can the infinite relate to the finite? How can the transcendent God be known by creatures? In Jesus, eternity enters time. The Creator stoops to be with His creation. God is not distant but present, not unknowable but revealed.

But the incarnation is not only a philosophical solution. It addresses the deepest needs of the human heart. The greatest obstacle to belief for many is the problem of evil. If God is good, why is there suffering? Here, the incarnation offers something no abstract deity can: a God who suffers with us. On the cross, Jesus bore pain, injustice, and death. He did not remain aloof but entered time and space and experienced our condition. In doing so, He provides both solidarity with us and salvation for us. We long for forgiveness and reconciliation. Our efforts fall dreadfully short. Only if God Himself bridges the gap can our sins be forgiven. The incarnation makes this possible.

When we put the pieces together, a remarkable picture emerges. Rational arguments show that God exists. Historical evidence shows that Jesus lived, died, and rose again. Philosophical reflection shows that only the incarnation fully explains God's nearness and love. Existentially, it offers meaning, hope, and redemption. These strands converge in one conclusion: Christianity is true.

V. Why "Beyond Reasonable Doubt"

In a courtroom, the highest standard of proof is "beyond reasonable doubt." It does not mean every possible doubt is eliminated—no human inquiry can achieve that. It means the evidence is so strong that any remaining doubts are unreasonable.

This is precisely the standard Christianity meets. Theism explains the origin of the universe, the design of nature, and the reality of morality better than atheism. The life, death, and resurrection of Jesus are among the best-attested events of ancient history. The coherence of the incarnation explains both philosophical questions and personal longings.

To reject this evidence is possible, but it requires more faith in improbable alternatives: that the universe came from nothing, that life and morality emerged by accident, that the resurrection appearances were illusions or lies. Such beliefs are not skeptical; they are credulous and defy the evidence. It is Christianity that stands beyond reasonable doubt.

VI. Conclusion

At the end of the day, the Christian claim is not merely that God exists or that Jesus lived long ago. It is that the Creator of the universe became flesh in order to save you. This is not wishful thinking but the most rational conclusion to draw from the evidence.

Yet Christianity is not simply an intellectual position to be affirmed. It is an invitation to trust. If Jesus is who He claimed to be—if He really rose from the dead—then He is not just a figure of history but the Lord of your life.

The evidence is before you. Beyond reasonable doubt, God is real, and He has revealed Himself in Jesus Christ. The verdict is clear. Moreover, God's verdict on you is clear. You did not choose Him, but He chose you. He chose you for life and salvation (John 15:16).

Who Am I

Rev. Merritt Demski

Who are you?

How do you usually answer that question? What comes to mind when you think about who you are?

Does your mind jump to things you do? Perhaps, the ways you feel? Or maybe, how you think about things? Or do you start with who Christ says you are?

We live in a culture that tells you to find your identity in your thoughts, feelings, and actions. We often think we are the sum of what we feel, think, and do. Someone asks, "Who are you?" and we say our name followed by something like, "I'm a basketball player." "I'm a musician…athlete…employee…student…comic geek." "I'm depressed…anxious…angry…confused…."

Our Creator points us in a different direction. He says we are sinners (Romans 3:23; James 2:10). Every human is conceived with a sinful nature that separates us from God (Psalm 51:5; Ephesians 2:1). God created all things good (Genesis 1:31), but humanity rebelled against God and brought sin into the world, which separated us from God who is the good source of life (Genesis 3).

But that's not the end of the story...or this would be a real bummer of an essay.

God promised that the seed of the woman would crush the serpent's head and the serpent would bruise the seed's heel (Genesis 3:15). God promised that the identity of humanity would not always be "dead people" or "condemned sinners."

God came in the flesh to give us a new identity (John 1:1, 14). God made us in the image of God, which was corrupted by sin, but God sent His Son, Jesus Christ, who IS the image of God (Colossians 1:15). God sent His Son to take your sins and my sins upon Himself and to take those sins all the way to God's wrath and punishment on the cross (John 3:16) fulfilling God's promises about the seed and the serpent.

Then God raised Jesus from the dead three days later (Acts 10:40). Now we are baptized into that death and resurrection (Romans 6). We are baptized into Christ, and so we are now "sons of God through Christ Jesus" (Galatians 3:26). Because Christ has kept the law and pleased God, we have been made pleasing in God's sight (Colossians 2:11-14). The image of Christ covers us.

When someone asks, "Who are you?" You can faithfully say, "I'm a baptized child of God who plays sports...music...goes to school...etc...."

Your identity is not found in how you feel, what you think, or the wrongs you've committed. Your identity has been given to you by your Creator and King. He brought you from death to life in His eternal kingdom (Romans 5; Ephesians 2).

You're not the sum of what you do, think, or feel. Your identity is rooted in the saving work of Jesus Christ. Yes, you have emotions. Yes, you have done things wrong. Yes, you have many thoughts. But the blood of Christ is greater. We take all of these things captive to Christ (2 Corinthians 10:4-6).

It's hard to remember that, though. It's hard not to get sidetracked by various ideas that float around the world (Ephesians 4:14). It's hard not to want to make a name for ourselves here and now. We like attention. We get distracted from the attention God gives to us and calls us to give to Him for the sake of the people around us (Hebrews 12:1-2).

We want to be the cool jock, or the knowledgeable scholar, or the interesting geek, but Christ calls you to be His child (Galatians 3:26), friend (James 2:23; James 4:4), servant/slave (Romans 6:22; John 8:36), citizen (Philippians 3:20; Hebrews 13:14; Ephesians 2:19), and so forth.

Scripture articulates our identity in Christ in these various ways. They are all glorious titles of who we are, and we must remember them always because if we don't know who we are, we won't know what to do.

All of this talk about who we are isn't supposed to be a mere therapeutic answer to our troubles. Knowing who you are isn't just supposed to make you cry less when someone calls you a name or when you do something wrong. It won't magically make stress in your life disappear. Yes, our identity in Christ gives us joy (Psalm 30:5), but it does so because it draws our eyes to a bigger picture. When our eyes are on Jesus, we remember that He'll wipe away every tear (Revelation 21:4) and the suffering we face now is nothing compared to the glory which is to come in Christ Jesus (Romans 8:18).

When we see who God has made us through the grace of Jesus Christ, we see that regardless of our life circumstances, Christ is with us (Matthew 28:20). Life will change, skills and abilities will come and go, there will be good times and bad times, but our identity in Christ will remain as the Holy Spirit keeps us in repentance and faith in Christ.

And when we remember that, we're able to do what God has called us to do.

He hasn't called you to simply sit with a smile, knowing that you'll be raised to eternal life when He returns again. He has called you to do good things in the name of Jesus (Ephesians 2:8-10; 2 Timothy 3:16-17).

Ephesians 2:8-10 says, "For by grace you have been saved through faith. And this is not your own doing; it is the gift of God, not a result of works, so that no one may boast. For we are his workmanship, created in Christ Jesus for good works, which God prepared beforehand, that we should walk in them."

You're saved by the grace of God...not your intellect or will. You're saved by grace through faith to be God's workmanship for good works. He prepared you to love God and love your neighbor

(Matthew 22:36-40). He forms you into the image of Jesus, into whom you've been baptized, so that you walk as He has called you to walk (Romans 8:29, 12:2; 2 Corinthians 3:18; Ephesians 4:11-15).

God has made you His own through Jesus. When you know that, the rest of the picture looks clearer. If we're only focused on this moment when we're doing well in band, on the field, or at the job, we lose sight of the eternal reality in Jesus. If we don't know who we are, we don't know what to do.

Who are you? You're a Christian. You've been baptized into the image of Christ, and you're fed with that image as you approach the Lord's Table. Your sins are forgiven, and you're reconciled with God. You're no longer focused on who you think you are but rather on who God has made you to be.

Jesus is always the point. We're baptized into His identity as the Son of God; thus, everything else we do must be shaped in that way (Romans 6).

We live as slaves to the Lord, doing His will. We live as citizens of God's Kingdom, obeying His good commands. We live as children of our heavenly Father as He provides for us, teaches us, and molds us into the image of Jesus.

Now that you're in Christ, you look at the whole world differently. You no longer look at the world asking, "What's in it for me?" You're looking at the world asking, "What has God called me to do with peace and joy in His service and in the service of others?"

The table of duties in the catechism functions for that exact purpose. "Oh, you're a citizen? Here's what it looks like to live like a citizen as a Christian." "You're a husband. Here's what your Lord calls you to in marriage." "You have parents. Here's how you should interact with them."

If our identity is rooted in ourselves, there's only going to be sorrow. "Yes, I'm a husband. That's who I am." Well, what if your wife passes away?

"I put all of my eggs in the basket of being a mother." If that's your only identity, then what about the loss of a child or transitioning into the days when the kids aren't around 24/7?

We keep Christ at the center of our lives to focus on who we are...in Christ.

To know who we are in Christ, we must know Jesus. We must know the one who is our Lord and King (1 Timothy 6:15...and tons in Revelation), Perfect God (John 1:1, 14), Perfect Man (1 Timothy 2:5; Philippians 2:7). We must know the one who suffered, the one who rose. If we don't know Him, we don't know who we are. God made us in His image, and now He calls us to be conformed to that image.

When we ask what God's will is, it is no longer rooted in our thoughts, emotions, and abilities. It's rooted in who Christ is and how we live in Christ. Keep Christ at the center rather than yourself so that you've got your eternal thoughts rightly ordered.

When we do that, our attention is in the right place. There may still be trials and difficulties, but in Christ, we'll have life and peace. We'll know what it looks like to be a man of God or a woman of God. We won't be crippled by questions like, "What now?" Instead, we'll be focused on the one into whom we've been baptized and who will return to bring us into eternal life (John 5:28-29).

We're made new in Christ. Our sins are forgiven. We have eternal life, but we don't see it yet. Our eyes don't see the fullness of God's promises even though they're true.

We live in this "now" and "not yet." The "not yet" gives us hope while we wait in the "now" for the "not yet."

It's hard to be patient and to walk in faith. Our sinful hearts, though drowned in Baptism, still rear their heads, saying, "Maybe you really are only an athlete. Maybe you are just a kid and there's nothing more. Maybe the feelings you have should be the most important things in your life and should rule over you."

In those times, we pray for strength against temptation (Matthew 26:41). We pray for Jesus to come quickly so we see who we are in Christ (Revelation 22:20). In the meantime, we are about the things of God. We gather to hear His word and to receive the Sacrament. We gather knowing that in Christ, we have eternal life.

In the face of all of the messages that the world gives, we look to the Lord's Word for guidance. We look forward to the resurrection. We don't fear death; we don't get sidetracked with sin and pleasure. We're focused on the joy of the Lord. When we sin and forget these things, we confess our sins and He's faithful to forgive (1 John 1). We're reminded week in and week out that in Christ we have forgiveness and everlasting life in Christ alone. Our grave is nothing. We get the resurrected Body and Blood of life to have eternal life by faith.

The burdens that you face now will be nothing compared to the glory that will be revealed in Christ Jesus. All of the messages of the world that burden your heart and soul, telling you you're not enough and that you failed again, get drowned out by the waters of God's Word in the waters of Baptism. Your weakness reveals Christ's strength as He brings you to His Father (2 Corinthians 12:9-11).

When we see the eternal picture, we see how little the problems that we face now are. We may think they're the biggest issues in the world if our identity and entire being are wrapped up in what we do, think, and feel, but when our identity is in Christ, who is the first and last who has already defeated death (Revelation 1), then we see we can truly walk with our feet fitted with the gospel of peace (Ephesians 6).

Sure, we work diligently, but we work in a state of readiness for Christ's return (1 Corinthians 15:52). We work knowing that at any time our identity in Christ may be revealed in its fullness. You are baptized into Christ, and you are called to walk in His footsteps. We suffer as He suffered. We love as He loves. We forgive as He forgives. We walk as Christ has called us to. We listen to Jesus. We hear His word of instruction and peace, and we go to Him for all that we need in repentance and faith.

We thank, praise, serve, and obey our Lord, knowing exactly who we are. We're baptized children of God through Jesus who have been forgiven by a loving and merciful Father who will bring us into glory on the Last Day when Christ returns again. Amen! Go in peace and serve the Lord!

All Things NEW

Rev. Randy Sturzenbecher

My dear struggling brothers and sisters in Christ:

I can't tell you the number of times I have wished for the end. Not my end, although there have been a few pretty low days and nights, but the end of my sin and the struggle it causes. I long for relief and peace for my family and friends as they suffer from diseases or are senselessly caught in the dysfunction and brokenness of the world.

It seems that more and more, the suffering and pain and disorder of so many things fight to become our new normal. When our phone buzzes, we are usually expecting the worst. Worry and anxiety always want to paralyze and control our thoughts, words, and actions. Selfish pride and self-promotion are encouraging us to crawl over someone else to get to the top rather than lending a hand to pull the struggling up. Silly arguments and snarky comments become the outlet for our discontentment. The old Adam continually thinks he knows better than God and incessantly tempts us to doubt God is good and loving and cares for us. My dear friends, there is hope in the darkness! There is hope in the chaos and brokenness of your life. We have the absolute assurance that Christ will once again come to make all things new and put an end to sin and death and the evil one's influence over us.

St. John writes in Revelation 21,

> "And I heard a loud voice from the throne saying, 'Behold, the dwelling place of God is with man. He will dwell with them, and they will be his people, and God himself will be with them as their God. He will wipe away every tear from their eyes, and death shall be no more, neither shall there be mourning, nor crying, nor pain anymore, for the former things have passed away.' And he who was seated on the throne said, 'Behold, I am making all things new.'"

Most of the time when we hear St. John and his Revelation of Jesus, we are thinking about "the end." Christ Jesus descends from heaven and stands upon the earth one final time. The dead burst forth from their narrow chambers as Jesus calls them from their rest. Creation is restored and in harmony. Soul and bodies are made new, never to be separated by death again. And if you and I are alive to see that wonderful and glorious day, we will be made new as well! I say and pray quite frequently, "Come Lord Jesus. Come quickly," because I am tired of the pain and suffering of being broken and living in a broken world.

What we can miss when we hear Jesus saying, "Behold, I am making all things new," is that He is making things new today, right now… for you. Jesus making things new for you today is to keep you grounded in His promises and give you eternal hope right now while things are still very broken.

Let's start where God started when He made you new the first time. For many of us, a pastor held you in his arms, said your name, poured water over your head in the Name of the Father and of the Son and of the Holy Spirit, and you were made new. You were regenerated and gifted faith to believe in His loving and eternal promises for you today in your brokenness. You were made new, not by any work of yours. Not because you deserved it, but because the triune God loved you from the beginning. An eternal adoption took place the day of your Baptism. An eternal, unchanging identity was given to you that day. Eternal promises were made to you that day. By simple water and the power of God's Word, you were connected to Good Friday. Jesus, God's only Son, willingly endured crucifixion and death so He could take from you what would separate you from your making-new Father. Your sin, your disobedience, and even your death were taken by Jesus before you were born so that you were made new on your Baptism day. On the cross, Jesus said, "Tetelestai," it is finished! Your sin, all of it finished. It has no power to condemn you or accuse you because the price for sin, which is death, was paid lovingly by Jesus. You are forgiven.

But wait...there is more! Resting in His borrowed grave, Jesus made holy the graves of all His Baptized who rest in the earth until He makes them new one last time. Before Resurrection morning, He descended into Hell, not as a punishment for being the sin-bearer of all humanity, but as our Victor over death and grave and all things evil. Imagine Jesus standing healthy and whole, bearing the nail and spear wounds of Satan's fatal attempt. Our old evil foe can't believe what he sees. This crucified man, who was lifeless on the cross and buried in a borrowed tomb, lives never to die again! And because Jesus died and lives again, so will you. You will be made new after death has momentarily done its worst. Satan's reign over you has been ended. Yes, he still howls and rages in the world, but he cannot undo what Christ has done for you on the cross. That, my friends, is our hope for the Last Day and every day until then.

Every time you are broken because of your sin, or simply caught in a broken situation, Satan would have you believe you are separated from God and any hope. That's a lie. But it is a lie that works well for Satan, so he keeps using it. Adam and Eve in the garden sinned, and then when God came to find them, they ran. They hid. They played the blame game, justifying themselves, all the while trying to separate from God because sin had now broken the sinless relationship between God and man. Fast forward to today. Is it any different in your world? Temptation lays the trap; your idol or idols, or your addiction, is more than happy to be satisfied. Temporary enjoyment and then the law does its killing work. Just like the prophet Nathan, who stood in front of King David and said, "You are the man!" The accusing finger of the law hits our hearts and conscience with the reality that "you are the man". You are the idolator, listening to the old Adam and running off to where the demons dwell. You are the mocker and despiser of authority. You are the thief, the liar, the stealer of reputations. You are the pornographer, the adulterer, and the breaker of marriage.

Once the law has done its accusing and killing work, Satan tries to drive the wedge of shame and guilt and embarrassment between you and your only hope, Jesus. He so subtly tries to convince you that it is easier to hide from God than confess to Him. Satan spins the guilt that you feel into an excuse to run away from God because sin and brokenness will always see God as the righteous Judge who only seeks to destroy.

Don't buy the lie. Don't believe that God is only out for retaliation and destruction. Look to the Cross. Look to Jesus. Look to the promise God gave to Adam and Eve immediately when sin began to separate. God would send Jesus to crush the head of the lying serpent, Satan, and be forgiveness for you.

The great deception that Satan spins is that God demands perfection from you alone. Yes, it is true that God will not tolerate any sin. But it is also true that God provided that perfection for you in His one and only Son. The Old Testament Prophet Isaiah pointed ahead with laser accuracy to Jesus. "Therefore, the Lord himself will give you a sign. Behold, the virgin shall conceive and bear a son and shall call his name Immanuel" (Isaiah 7:14). "For to us a child is born, to us a son is given; and the government shall be upon his shoulder, and his name shall be called Wonderful Counselor, Mighty God, Everlasting Father, Prince of Peace" (Isaiah 9:6). "Surely, He has borne our griefs and carried our sorrows; yet we esteemed him stricken, smitten by God, and afflicted. But he was pierced for our transgressions; he was crushed for our iniquities; upon him was the chastisement that brought us peace, and with his wounds we are healed" (Isaiah 53:4-6).

Dear Saints, don't buy the lie of the deceiver that always seeks to divide and separate you from hope. Look to your promised Redeemer and Lord. Look to Jesus and His compassion and forgiveness. Hear His forgiveness pronounced to you by your pastor in the Divine Service. If you still struggle with Satan's lies, go see your pastor in individual Confession and Absolution and let him speak Jesus directly to your fear and doubt and sin. Let him remind you through God's Word of the hope that is yours this day, right now, because of

Jesus. You are forgiven. You are made new again as your pastor lays his hands on your head and says, "In the stead and by the command of my Lord Jesus Christ, I forgive you all your sins in the name of the Father and of the Son and of the Holy Spirit. Amen." Jesus draws near to you with His Gifts of Word and Sacrament to forgive you. No sin is stronger than Jesus. No brokenness is so bad that Jesus would deny you hope, peace, and forgiveness. No sin is so devastating that Jesus would reject you. He died for all of them. He died for you to be forgiven and made new. Yes, you may be experiencing the temporal consequences of your sin. But even in that, you, as a Baptized child of God, drawing near to Jesus, trusting Him to hear your confession, have forgiveness declared to you by the authority of Jesus the Christ, the living Son of the Father. Even if the situation you are in is still completely broken, the love and forgiveness of Jesus is for you right there in the dysfunctional disaster you call your life.

This wonderful, making all things new hope that we have in Jesus seems hard to believe. In fact, without faith it is impossible to believe. So, God gives us everything we need. He gives faith in Baptism. He connects us to the Cross through faith. He gives us the gift of forgiveness and peace because Jesus' blood covers all our sin. That is yours right now!

There are a lot of other views in your world that would have you believe something other than what Jesus says. Dear Saints, let the promises of God's Word strengthen you when the divergent messages in the world try to cause you to doubt. Remember these promises from Revelation 21. "Behold, the dwelling place of God is with man." Not just at the end of all things when Jesus comes again, but right now. He is in His Holy Word. He is in His Supper. He dwells in you, His made-new creation.

Here is your hope for today. "He will wipe away every tear from their eyes, and death shall be no more, neither shall there be mourning, nor crying, nor pain anymore, for the former things have passed away" (Revelation 21:4). Yes, all of that will happen one last time when Jesus returns. But all of that is yours now, right in the middle of all the broken, hope shines brightly. Your tears of regret and shame were wiped away by the forgiveness of your sin.

"Death shall be no more" because Jesus died your death. St. Paul assures us in Romans 6 that "if we have been united with him in a death like his, we shall certainly be united with him in a resurrection like His." Jesus rose from death, and so will you because you are His.

"Neither shall there be mourning, nor crying, nor pain anymore, for the former things have passed away." For right now, on this side of the resurrection of all flesh, mourning and crying and pain still exist because sin is still breaking things. But they do not consume us or control us or leave us hopeless. Even in your brokenness, Jesus is there forgiving you, strengthening you, and giving you hope! Remember this every day, dear struggling one.

"Behold, I am making all things new."

Aaron Fenker

Dust and ashes. Dead and gone. That's how everyone ends up. We weren't created that way, but it was the curse levied against the first king of humanity, Adam. It was the curse for his rebellion—"Dust you are, and to dust you shall return" (Genesis 3:19). Each generation has taken up that rebellion. Each as king and queen of our own universe selfishly rebels against God, and so "death spread to all men because all sided." Dust and ashes. Dead and gone. That'll be you someday.

Dust and ashes. That's every single kingdom, empire, and nation of the world. None of their rulers lived forever. None of their power, influence, and control lasted all that long, all things considered. Crumbled walls. Failed rules. Dead dynasties. And sure, maybe some monuments, statues, and roads are left, but they're all empty of their former glory. Who really knows why those people are important anyway, and their dead-end roads to nowhere? Dust and ashes.

Dust and ashes. That's the church, too. Failed programs. Dwindling choirs. Scant membership. Crumbling steeples. Shuttered doors. Yes, the church is dust and ashes. Abandon all hope ye who enter the church, our detractors say. Despair. It's hopeless. The devil's set against us. The world and the kingdoms of this world are or will persecute us. And even you and I, who really wants to go to a place like that? Who really wants to be a pastor in such a place? The reality is the church isn't just dying. It's dead. It's dead and gone. It's dust and ashes. Yes, the church really is dust and ashes—in our hands.

That's a tough pill to swallow. That's our repentance. But maybe you're a bit confused, or perhaps you disagree. But here's the thing: Your soup supper won't save your congregation. If the church is just a gathering of like-minded individuals, if the church is just potlucks, social gatherings, all diamonds and card playing, if the church is just soup kitchens, homeless shelters, pregnancy support centers, then the church and your congregation will last just as long as you can keep it going. Someday, maybe sooner, maybe later, you or your children or your grandchildren will shutter the doors of that church for the last time. It'll just be a mausoleum, a museum, all the accomplishments of its members. Or maybe your church becomes the hot ticket in town, known as the best at whatever, gathering bustling members, growing groups here, there, and everywhere, that dear friend is just a whitewashed tomb. A church dead while she lives.

None of those things are the Church. Oh, they may be part of a church we set up, but they're not part of the Church. The church we set up is dust and ashes in our hands, but the church, the true Church, the real church, isn't in your hands or mine. The real church is in the hands of Jesus. Little "c" church isn't just dust and ashes. It's already dead and gone! That's not just a dying church but a dead church. But big "C" Church is in the nail-scarred hands of Jesus. So, she's living and active and shall live forever because he lives forever.

The true and living church is not ashes. It's the opposite of dust and ashes! It's a fertile field always blossoming, always blooming, always growing. The true church isn't some heap of smoldering rubble. The true church is glorious and splendid without spot, wrinkle, or any such thing because Christ has made her so. She is his bride. The Church isn't some sort of zombie institution, but it is the living body of Christ, and we are members of His body (Ephesians 5).

The Church is fertile and green—a vibrant marshland, enlivened by the living waters of Holy Baptism. Christ says that the Kingdom of God is like a mustard tree, under whose branches all the birds come to roost (Matthew 13). The Church is also like a comforting willow, by which she takes after her Lord, the blessed man who's like a tree planted by living waters (Psalm 1).

The Church is satisfying and sustaining because she is satisfied and sustained by the only thing that endures through the ages. Where are the individual cities or congregations where the prophets and apostles preached the Word of God? Nowhere but the holy Christian and apostolic Church, the Church scattered across the world, is built on the foundation of the prophets and the Apostles, Christ Himself being the Cornerstone, ever endures, is ever strong, is everlasting. She is always expanding and growing because of Christ's Word. After all, "the grass withers and the flower fades, but the Word of God endures forever." Yet, it's not just any word of God: "This Word is the Gospel that has been preached to you" (1 Peter 1).

The Gospel ever and always gives life to the Church and each one of her members. It can't *not* give life! As the Lord says: "For as the rain and the snow come down from heaven and do not return there but water the earth, making it bring forth and sprout, giving seed to the sower and bread to the eater, so shall my word be that goes out from my mouth; it shall not return to me empty, but it shall accomplish that which I purpose, and shall succeed in the thing for which I sent it" (Isaiah 55). His Word in the Church always grants you light, revelation, life, vibrancy, and blessing. "For it is the God who commanded light to shine out of darkness, who has shone in our hearts to give the light of the knowledge of the glory of God in the face of Jesus Christ" (2 Corinthians 4).

The Church is the Vineyard of God, where Christ is the Vine, and we are the branches. Christ Himself shares His life with us. Apart from Him, we can do nothing (John 15). A true branch of Christ is any believer who remains in Christ in him and he in Christ. (That branch, of course, bears much fruit.) But that branch—you and I and every true member (believer) of the Christian Church—remains in Christ and Christ in him by virtue of His flesh and blood. Whoever eats His flesh and drinks His blood remains in Christ and Christ in him, has eternal life, and Christ will resurrect Him on the Last Day. (John 6) After all, "we are members of His body," the Church, "of His flesh and of His bones" (Ephesians 6).

If you look at the Church with worldly eyes, she's useless, meaningless. What use does the world have for such a weak institution?

It's better left marginalized. And church, as we set it up, is worse than that. It's dead. There's no hope, present or future, for that kind of church. The only hope for the Church of Christ is not its programs or its balanced budgets. The hope for the Church is not its members or its current and future youth. The hope isn't demographics or immigration trends. The only hope is the only hope any one of us has—JESUS Christ, who rose victorious over sin, death, Satan, and Hell on the Third Day.

The dead and risen Christ knows well how to govern, guard, and save His Church. Left in our hands, the church is DOA, but in Christ's nail-scarred hands, it's alive and living forever. And the future hope for the Church rests with His almighty power to save, which He exercises through His Word and Baptism and His Supper. Through these, He makes His Church a vibrant marshland, a sustained and well-built fortress, and an ever-living vine grafted into Him by faith. We believe this to be true. It's our only hope—Christ is our only hope.

He gives us all these things. He uses us to proclaim His salvation from day to day, to proclaim to a dead and dying world the excellencies of Him who brought us out of darkness into His marvelous light (1 Peter 2). He will use each of us, according to His good and gracious will, to call all people to repentance and faith in Him, which happens where and when it pleases God the Holy Spirit, in those who hear the gospel, who are Baptized, who are absolved, and who receive Communion.

Because of Christ alone, by His almighty Word and salutary Gifts alone, can we believe, teach, and confess that one holy Church is to remain forever. The Church is the congregation of saints in which the gospel is purely taught and the Sacraments are correctly administered. That Church will remain forever, even though her members will die and rise. And one day very soon Christ will return, and on that Day every eye will see Him—you and I, too—face to face in endless joy. And we shall also see "the holy city, new Jerusalem, coming down out of heaven from God, prepared as a bride adorned for her husband" (Revelation 21:2).

Then the promise of God will be fulfilled forever: "Behold, the dwelling place of God is with man. He will dwell with them, and they will be his people, and God himself will be with them as their God. He will wipe away every tear from their eyes, and death shall be no more, neither shall there be mourning, nor crying, nor pain anymore, for the former things have passed away" (Revelation 21:4). Dust and ashes will pass away, but you will rise and live forever. The Church will endure forever, for Her Husband, your Lord and Savior Jesus Christ has died and risen forever, "never to die again, death has no more dominion over Him" (Romans 6). He alone is the risen Hope of His Church—yours, too!

Conclusion

For 25 years, Higher Things has gathered youth from coast to coast and everywhere in between. From Atlantic to Pacific to Gulf, to the great plains and great lakes. From towering forests to the heartland, and cities and towns, Higher Things has strived to clearly proclaim the Gospel to youth and young adults, to dare them to be Lutheran, to show them that their salvation was won for them by Jesus Christ on the Cross.

Whether we learned what it meant to be Dying To Live in Wyoming, traveled to the City of God, Seattle, sang the Te Deum in Las Vegas, heard the FOR YOU in Minneapolis, Asheville, Bozeman, Valparaiso, and every other conference site, we were reminded that we are Watermarked in baptism while we were all sitting in front of our computer screens, rejoiced that in All Things new and the resurrection in Amherst, and learned that Dying Church Rising Hope is exactly how God wants it to be in St. Louis. Through 25 conference themes, Higher Things has boldly clung to the cross of Christ. We're still teaching.

This collection of 26 essays celebrates each of our conferences as we reflect upon the whole counsel of God, bit by bit, year by year. Written by the presenter, the preacher, the group leader, the attendee, the staff member, these essays reflect why Higher Things not only chose the theme, but why Higher Things continues to return to each of the themes in everything we do, and why Higher Things's mission to make the Gifts of Christ Jesus known to youth and young adults knows no timeframe.

Soli Deo Gloria

Higher Things is blessed to celebrate our 25th anniversary. Since our first conference, we have taught what it means to be ***Dying to Live***, and we've been ***Making Waves*** ever since. Higher Things exists to make the Gifts of Christ known to youth and young adults, reminding them that they are always ***In His Face***. We've traveled throughout North America to the ***Cities of God***, ***Daring to be Lutheran***. Our resources have reached all across the world. We've stood at the altar with thousands of youth for ***The Feast***, and we've always kept Christ crucified ***For You*** on the lips of every speaker. We strive to remind them of their Baptism and point them to the Cross. We don't water down our content—we challenge youth. We know they will rise to the task. We have said ***Amen*** in churches, chapels, ballrooms, theaters, and field houses. We seek to assist their parents, pastors, and congregations in the formation of their faith, teaching the next generation the Gospel of Jesus Christ: that they are saved by grace alone, through faith alone, as revealed in Scripture alone—the ***Sola***s. We work when we work, we worship when we worship, and we play when we play. We have been ***Given*** a great task: to remind young people that they will always be ***Coram Deo***, before God, and that they are disciples just like the ***Twelve*** who traveled with Christ from Galilee to Jerusalem. We only wish to teach them of the one, true God who came ***From Above***, and was ***Crucified*** for our sins. Singing out in multitudes, ***Te Deum*** Laudamus, God, we praise you. Twenty-five years is just the beginning for Higher Things. We will continue to do more, create more, produce more, and teach more. We will persevere in our commitment to youth and young adults so that those attending today will remain firmly planted in their faith and teach the next generation. We will continue to dare youth to be Lutheran and have a blast while doing it! We have given the true ***Bread of Life*** to thousands of youth, adults, parents, and pastors—proclaiming just like Luther at Worms: ***Here I Stand***. Reminding—teaching—that all are ***Sanctified*** in Christ. In ***Concordia***, we sing. In Concordia, we remember that we are ***Watermarked*** at the font, and ***Forgiven*** all our sins, all on account of Christ. That's what it's all about... Christ crucified ***For You***. This fact we proclaim to the youth, young adults, parents, pastors, and leaders- ***Beyond Reasonable Doubt***. When our youth ask the question, ***Who Am I?*** We loudly proclaim with the entire bride of Christ, "a baptized child of God." When the world around them and their burdens become too much, when it seems that all hope is lost, we loudly proclaim that we have faith in a resurrection that will make ***All Things New.*** We look forward with hope in this resurrection. As we celebrate this 25th anniversary, we see the once-plentiful church spires around us crumbling, attendance numbers dwindling, and the "remember when" whispers abound. We say something else—consider yourself dead to sin and alive to God in Christ Jesus. Look around. The Word is preached faithfully. The Sacraments are administered rightly. This is how it's supposed to be. ***Dying Church… Rising Hope***